Introduction

Generally, when you say "pot," what comes to a great many people's psyches is getting out the smoking stuff and illuminating some. That is generally normal these days.

Back then, at that point, however, individuals just ate cannabis. I'm discussing individuals from

old times. They would utilize pot seeds in their food, and the blossoms loaded with pitch were for profound, therapeutic, and sporting purposes. There's an old-fashioned formula - maybe the most established one - which is called bhang. We have India to thank for bhang, a blend of almonds, milk, garam masala, and marijuana. It's normally taken during the excellent celebration of Holi, which is of Hindu beginning. It is a festival of Shiva, who is purportedly a divinity in affection with cannabis.

There is additionally Islamic writing, which shows pot utilization is the same old thing. In One Thousand and One Nights, there are two or three weed eaters. Even the legendary Dumas and Baudelaire took part in the herb, by mixing hashish — the purest form of cannabis — into their coffee.

Here in America, we have weed colors. These colors are the dynamic elements of the marijuana plant in a dissolvable structure, and up till late during the 1800s, it was promptly accessible in your neighborhood drug store. Smoking Heaven's spice didn't turn into a thing until ahead of schedule in the twentieth century.

I go over this since I need to clarify that eating the spice is the same old thing. It is a practice. It's old, and consecrated, and goes far back even past history. I was trusting you could consider consuming weed something mending to your body, providing it with supplements, feeding it.

I should bring up this since I don't need you becoming tied up with the untruths and promulgation that have plagued this awesome spice for a really long time, essentially due to the nearsighted perspective on the individuals who have been in power from the mark of first experience with this nation, till now.

The marijuana plant is completely innocuous. For a really long time, research showing its advantage had been constantly smothered by the people who might have had a ton to lose by allowing this plant to be openly accessible to you and me. Fortunately, that is changing.

Chances are you've had a pot brownie, or you have a companion or two who have attempted it. It was presumably the main way they ate marijuana. These wonderful brownies have been a thing since the 50s, permitting individuals to live it up at the motion pictures, as they camp, or paying attention to extraordinary music at shows. You can thank an individual dauntless extremist in '92 named Brownie Mary, who constantly got captured for serving her chocolate treats to San Francisco AIDs patients. Chocolate brownies have remained extremely

well known over any remaining strategies for eating the plant since chocolate is phenomenal at covering the flavor of cannabis.

By the time the 1960s and 1970s moved around, food turned into a tremendous piece of the pot world, particularly as the hipsters of that time went veggie lover, deciding to eat things like ocean growth, tofu, hummus, lentils, curries, falafel, arepas, and burritos. They simply needed something to eat that was not counterfeit, enclosed by plastic, or prepackaged and loaded with added substances and additives. I realize a great many people likely accept that all stoners are into lousy nourishment, yet I guarantee you that is only more publicity. Regardless, there is a monstrous measure of stoners worried about practicing good eating habits, nutritious food, as the spice places you in contact with your body and what it needs, making you search out better choices.

By virtue of the progressive legitimization of weed, many individuals have come to acknowledge it is much preferable to eat their marijuana over to smoke it. Thusly, they can keep their lungs solid and clean, don't need to manage the waiting smell of the tacky stuff or smoke on the face, hands, and garments, and can partake in the spice attentively any place they may be, regardless of whether it was at this point illicit to have marijuana in a portion of those places... Now, all things considered, I am not requesting that you violate the law. I'm only letting you know the reasons individuals started to ingest maryjane, as opposed to smoking it.

When you eat marijuana, you will observe that the impacts are unimaginably unique, since you're retaining all compounds through your stomach related framework, rather than your lungs. While it hits quicker when you smoke it when you eat it, you will find that your high requires a significant stretch of time to kick in, however when it does, it goes on for quite a while and influences both your brain and body.

Today, you will observe that weed is mixed into a wide range of dishes. Cooking with maryjane has turned into a madly aggressive field! There are so many astounding dishes you can make with pot, and I can hardly wait to impart them to you. If you're ready for a beautiful world rich in flavor and heavenly sensations, then you're in for a treat! Here's hoping you enjoy these recipes!

Chapter 1:   Cooking Cannabis is Legal

If you live in the United States, you might realize that there has been a push for the sanctioning of Marijuana in many states. The primary justification behind the push is drawn from the way that THC and CBD give numerous medical advantages. Some might contend that those pushing for legitimization are solely after the vibe great experience. In all actuality, there are many demonstrated medical advantages of both THC and CBD.

The new push for authorization has acquired a few achievement and aided push the legitimization of CBD and THC in certain states. It is legitimate to sell and consume CBD items in 50 conditions of the US. In many nations, there are no lawful limitations against CBD items. Any eatable that contains under 0.3% of THC won't cause you any lawful issues.

For this explanation, the vast majority are engaging in the development of CBD edibles. All things considered, some CBD edibles might contain more elevated levels of THC. It is now when you need to consider your nearby legislations.

If you plan to make CBD or THC edibles, I will suggest that you check with your neighborhood regulations. There are sure nations where possessing CBD or THC might prompt an extensive prison term or heavy fines. Albeit most nations are as yet working around CBD and THC's legalities, it is crucial to guarantee that you get explicit necessities for planning such edibles in your area. It is significantly more critical on the off chance that you plan to offer your palatable to other people.

Where Is It Legal To Use and Trade CBD and THC Products?

The subject of legitimizing weed has been drawn closer in two ways. The greater part of the individuals who contend for authorizing will generally underscore on its therapeutic worth. This has prompted where pot use must be ordered into sporting and clinical. In numerous nations, clinical weed has been authorized. Nonetheless, the utilization of weed for sporting intentions is liable to discussion.

When we talk about sporting pot, we principally allude to the immediate utilization of cannabis for individual joy. The vast majority who take weed for sporting purposes do as such through smoking. In this book, we don't advocate for the smoking of weed in any capacity. There are many wellbeing impacts related with smoking weed. Whenever you smoke, synthetic compounds from cannabis are probably going to influence your lungs and wreck with your breathing system.

To comprehend the legalities of weed in your state or country, you should comprehend the distinctions among sporting and restorative use. In most countries, using cannabis extracts such as THC or CBD is termed as medicinal. This additionally relies upon the sums consumed and the reason for consumption.

If you live in a nation where the sporting utilization of pot has been legitimized, you are more averse to fall into any instigating CBD or THC edibles. Notwithstanding, assuming you are in a nation or a state where just restorative maryjane has been authorized, you want to attempt to observe more data before you get into making edibles.

Here are nations where cannabis is legitimized, and you can make any kind of weed edibles.

United States

The US is one of the nations that has had a long fight with activists to sanction pot. With that being the situation, the individuals who advocate for marijuana and its items have to some extent won the war.

The subject of sanctioning weed items has been taken care of by each state, prompting to some degree mistaking lawful terms for the US. By and large, there are 11 states where pot has been legitimized both for clinical and sporting purposes. Further, there 22 states where pot has just been sanctioned for therapeutic purposes.

Here is a rundown of the states where you can plan CBD edibles. In states where weed is just legitimate for therapeutic purposes, you might get ready CBD edibles yet not THC edibles.

Alabama	Arizona-Recreational	Arkansas-Recreational	Connecticut-Recreational
Delaware-Recreational	Florida-Recreational	Georgia	Hawaii-Recreational
Indiana	Iowa	Kentucky	Louisiana-Recreational
Maryland-	Minnesota-	Mississippi	Missouri-

Recreational	Recreational		Recreational
Montana-Recreational	New Hampshire-Recreational	New Jersey-Recreational	New Mexico-Recreational
New York-Recreational	North Carolina	North Dakota-Recreational	Ohio-Recreational
Oklahoma-Recreational	Pennsylvania-Recreational	South Carolina	Tennessee
Texas	Utah- Recreational	Virginia	West Virginia-Recreational
Wisconsin	Wyoming		

Canada

Canada authorized sporting maryjane on seventeenth October 2018. This implies that you can plan both CBD and THC edibles assuming you are in Canada.

Mexico

It is legitimate to utilize sporting weed to sums under 5 grams. This implies that restorative pot isn't unlawful. Assuming you live in Mexico, you can feel free to get ready CBD and THC edibles.

Argentina

In March 2017, Argentina sanctioned restorative Marijuana. This intends that, assuming you are in Argentina, you can plan CBD edibles. Have a go at diving further into your exploration to comprehend the legalities around THC edibles in this country.

Jamaica

Jamaica is one of the nations where pot has been sanctioned for quite a while. Assuming you are in Jamaica, you ought to appreciate cooking and serving your CBD, THC, and hemp edibles.

Belgium

In Belgium, you can partake in weed as long as you are over the age of 18. Albeit sporting cannabis is legitimate, you can utilize around 3 grams. Assuming you are in Belgium, you can get ready THC and CBD edibles without a problem.

With that said, the prerequisites are severe on the sum consumed. Now and again, CBD oils might have a higher grouping of THC than the suggested 3 grams. In such a case, you need to set up your edibles with

less CBD oil to diminish THC.

Netherlands

In the Netherlands, it has been legitimate to partake in ganja in cafés for quite a while. In 2017, lawmakers changed the law to permit a few ranchers to establish marijuana. In such a country, you are not liable to cause problems for planning CBD or THC Products, in spite of the fact that I will suggest that you check with your neighborhood authorities.

Spain

For quite a while, there has been smoking clubs in Spain, yet they worked illicitly. In 2017, the Northern piece of Spain (Catalonia) sanctioned the utilization of sporting pot. On the off chance that you live in these pieces of Spain, you might make any THC or CBD edibles without an issue. In any case, for the individuals who live in southern Spain, you need to accomplish more digging.

Portugal

Portugal permits you to utilize and exchange maryjane or some other medication. In 2001, the state decriminalized all drugs. This implies that you can utilize any sort of medication without the danger of prison time. Be that as it may, you might confront fines or be taken to a treatment community assuming you are utilizing drugs excessively. Fundamentally, nothing bad can be said about consuming negligible measures of THC or CBD in your cookies.

Russia

This may appear to be out of nowhere, yet it is valid. Russia has authorized the utilization of weed as much as 6 grams. This implies that setting up your THC or CBD edibles ought not be a major problem.

Many different nations permit the utilization of pot for sporting purposes. The rundown of nations that permit the utilization of pot for therapeutic intentions is perpetual. Generally, it is only a modest bunch of nations that have a complete restriction on pot items. A portion of the nations where you might cause problems for getting ready CBD and THC edibles include:

Finland

France

Brazil

Chile

Japan

Lebanon

Malaysia

Kenya

Oman

UAE, among others

Chapter 2:   Benefits and Disadvantages of Using Cannabis-Based Foods

Although the health benefits of marijuana are auspicious, marijuana is by no means a miracle cure. It is essential to proceed with medicines recommended by your PCP and not make any impulsive moves until an educated doctor clears you. Marijuana can without a doubt assist with a few indications of genuine infections, similar to various sclerosis, epilepsy, and Parkinson's sickness, however there is no clinical proof that pot can fix any illness. In spite of the fact that researchers are hopeful that weed will demonstrate to assist with treating numerous significant sicknesses, and maybe much proposition a fix, there is a requirement for more clinical studies.

Recent exploration recommends a wide scope of clinical applications for marijuana. Concentrates on show it can assist with combatting manifestations like queasiness, torment, and tension from glaucoma, irritation, muscle fits, cerebral pains and headaches, absence of craving, restlessness, uneasiness, and wretchedness. A few investigations recommend that it can even stop the spread of malignant growth cells and slow the movement of Alzheimer's illness; examination into these areas is ongoing.

Finding out assuming pot is appropriate for you is an interaction that requires some investment. Assuming you have an ailment that marijuana is accounted for to help, talk with a clinical expert with regards to beginning the process.

Benefits

You can't ingest too much of weed. In pot's extended history, there has been no record of a deadly excess (contrast that with the six individuals every day who are killed by liquor harming or the 40 individuals every day who are killed by solution pain reliever overdose).

There are less unfavorable secondary effects. A few doctor prescribed medications have frightful incidental effects that can prompt sickness, congestive cardiovascular breakdown, coronary episodes, stroke, malignant growth, actual weakness, and even death.

The expense is low. Remedies can be very costly, and keeping in mind that you actually need to pay for clinical weed, it is without a doubt more reasonable than most physician endorsed drugs. With a green thumb and a little arrangement cost, you can even become your own medicine.

It helps your digestion. Late investigations exhibit a connection between pot use and a lower level of muscle versus fat. Results tracked down the pace of heftiness and diabetes to be significantly diminished in weed clients contrasted with non-weed users.

It safeguards your mind. Current science has distinguished the possible neuroprotective nature of marijuana, particularly concerning liquor prompted cerebrum harm. In sharp difference to the conviction that pot kills synapses, cannabinoids have, in certain cases, been related with the insurance and age of mind cells.

It can calm agony. Maryjane can diminish constant agony, especially neuropathic torment, which is nerve-related or famously difficult to treat with standard analgesics.

You can utilize it to unwind. Weed can loosen up your body and psyche, which is useful while treating a sleeping disorder, nervousness, and PTSD.

It builds hunger. The cannabinoid THC invigorates your craving, making it incredible for medical issue that make an absence of hunger and lead physical weakness.

It decreases sickness. Alongside expanding craving, weed decreases sickness. Patients going through chemotherapy need to keep their solidarity up, however eating might be the last thing they need to do. Marijuana can invigorate their hunger by decreasing nausea.

Disadvantages

Your manner of thinking and engine coordination can become impeded. High portions of THC might make debilitations transient memory, equilibrium, and coordination. Never drive or work large equipment while utilizing cannabis.

You can encounter dry mouth. One of the most well-known results of maryjane use is feeling like you have a lot of cotton balls in your mouth. Keep a beverage or ice pop handy!

It can build your hunger. Marijuana is recommended for patients with an absence of craving or queasiness, since, indeed, it builds your hunger. This may not be a welcome secondary effect, notwithstanding, on the off chance that you as of now have a sound appetite.

It briefly builds pulse. Assuming you have heart issues, talk with your primary care physician prior to sedating with pot. An expanded pulse may increase your danger of a heart attack.

Hallucinations can happen. Weed is a gentle hallucinogenic. High dosages of THC might cause hear-able or visual hallucinations.

You might feel tension, doubt, and frenzy. High dosages of weed or even moderate portions of certain strains might prompt these gloomy sentiments. In any case, pot can likewise diminish anxiety.

There are erratic impacts from one strain to another. Various strains might influence you in various ways, and a similar strain might be unique in relation to one cultivator to the next.

Inhalation of tar and synthetic compounds can be unsafe. Breathing in smoke from pot brings destructive tar and synthetics into the lungs and throat. While long haul studies haven't observed a relationship between's smoking marijuana and lung harm, patients with touchy or debilitated lungs or throat ought to stay away from smoking.

Long-term impacts are hazy. Current exploration has highlighted a few unimaginable advantages of marijuana, yet concentrates on miss the mark on long haul impacts of the different weed use methods.

Cannabis use is governmentally illicit. The central government boycotts marijuana. Utilizing it might put you in danger for lawful action.

Not much is been aware of the impacts of blending professionally prescribed medications and cannabis. On account of certain antidepressants, marijuana can expand unwanted incidental effects like tension, queasiness, and quick pulse. With antipsychotics, the very manifestations being dealt with might be aggravated with the utilization of weed. Once more, there is almost no examination on the blending of pot with doctor prescribed medications. If all else fails, talk with your doctor.

Other Health Benefits

Health Benefits of Cannabis

The utilization of weed for sporting purposes consistently developed from 1850-1930. With the expansion in the utilization of this medication, the public authority chose to characterize weed as a Schedule I drug under the Controlled Substances Act of 1970. This prompted an increment in the contentions that encompassed the therapeutic advantages that weed offers. THC at last got the endorsement of the US Food and Drug Administration in 1985. The US government additionally supported a review in 1999 into the advantages of weed and how it helps

certain circumstances. This study was attempted by the Institute of Medicine and showed that weed lessens the secondary effects achieved by chemotherapy. Beginning around 1999, there have been different investigations aimed at demonstrating the medical advantages that pot offers. Indeed, California was the principal state to sanction the utilization of clinical maryjane in 1966 and since

Slows Down Cancer

Prevention of Alzheimer's

Treating Glaucoma Reducing

Arthritis Control Epileptic

Seizures Soothing Tremors

Quitting Smoking and Drug Withdrawal

Anxiety Disorders

Reduces the Side Effects of Hepatitis C Reducing

the Side Effects of Chemotherapy Acne

Diabetes

Fibromyalgia

Chapter 3:   Main Ingredients Used

Cannabis Oil (How to make it from Marijuana)

Methods of Extraction

There are two essential techniques for removing CBD and THC at home. In spite of the fact that there are a few modern techniques for extraction, we won't zero in on modern options.

Solvent Extraction (Alcohol or Oil)

In the dissolvable extraction process, we will utilize a fluid dissolvable that can break down pot. As we have effectively noticed, marijuana is water phobic. This implies that water isn't the best decision assuming you are hoping to separate marijuana. Pot can either be broken up in liquor or other oils.

If you will utilize oil, look for a transporter oil of your decision. The usually utilized oils are coconut and olive. You can utilize different choices as well, as indicated by your inclinations. You likewise need to look for marijuana buds, either new or dried. In the readiness processes, we utilize decarboxylated buds. Regardless of whether you purchase dry or new, guarantee that they are decarboxylated before you start the cycle. Assuming you purchase new buds, you can decarboxylate them through the fast broiler process. In this interaction, you just spread the buds on a stove plate and spot them in your broiler 205 degrees F for 20-25 minutes.

Olive Oil CBD/THC Oil Extraction

Tools and Ingredients:

A hardened steel cooking pot

Olive oil-You may likewise involve liquor for the

equivalent. CBD/THC rich marijuana buds

Water

Directions:

In the cooking pot, blend one cup of olive oil in with one cup of water and switch on low hotness.

Assuming you are utilizing crude decarboxylated buds, simply guarantee that they are cut into little pieces. In the event that you are utilizing dried marijuana buds, you ought not have any issue, use them simply the way they are.

Add your weed buds to the water and oil blend while warming. Tenderly increment the temperature until you begin to notice slow bubbles.

Once rises begin appearing, diminish your hotness and slow cook the combination for around 30 minutes.

The ideal temperature for bubbling olive oil is 200 degrees C to guarantee that the oil doesn't dissipate, keep up with your temperature in the scope of 180 - 220 degrees F.

Once you see pot buds drifting over the water, switch off the hotness and let the blend sit undisturbed for around 3 minutes.

Once the blend chills off, strainer the oil through a fine channel into a dim glass and store it in a cool place.

The CBD oil got through this cycle is somewhere in the range of 40 and 60 percent strong assuming you utilized hemp buds. Assuming you are focusing to get THC oil, you can in any case utilize the very interaction with the exception of that you need to utilize marijuana buds. For THC oil, the intensity can be anyplace somewhere in the range of 10 and 3o percent. THC is an exceptionally inebriating substance. Any oil with an intensity of 10% or more can be potent.

If you are hoping to utilize unadulterated CBD or THC segregate, you should purchase from the market. Home readiness techniques don't permit us to make unadulterated CBD disconnect. In any case, you can work on the strength of your CBD oil through distillation.

CO2 CBD Extraction

Besides the dissolvable extraction strategy, both CBD and THC oils can be extricated through a CO2 technique. The CO2 strategy is more exact and offers profoundly powerful oils. Be that as it may, the technique is excessively convoluted and ought to just be finished by specialists. A great many people utilize the dissolvable technique above at home since the CO2 strategy requires costly equipment.

In the CO2 extraction process, exceptionally compressed CO2 is utilized to separate CBD and THC from pot buds. The cycle is known as the chilly extraction process, albeit the temperatures differ. In the extraction technique, there are three choices accessible. You can either utilize the subcritical, supercritical, or mid basic choices. These are for the most part processes inside the CO2 extraction approach not set in stone by the temperature of the process.

The CO2 cold press machine does CO2 extraction. Since the machines are excessively costly, you ought to just pick this choice for the business creation of CBD oil.

Even however you can't remove CBD or THC through the CO2 interaction, you could in any case purchase the oil from enormous makers. CBD and THC oils extricated through the virus cycle will quite often be more strong and cleaner than those acquired through the dissolvable interaction. Assuming you are searching for CO2 extricated oil, I will suggest buying from organizations that produce in huge quantities.

Making CBD/THC Oil from Cannabis Isolate

Various forms of cannabis and determined that cannabis isolates such as wax and hash have the highest potency. These disengages likewise give you a possibility for planning CBD or THC oil at home. On the off chance that you don't approach weed buds, simply purchase any marijuana confine from the market and use it to set up your oil for food preparation.

Ingredients:

- Pure CBD/THC isolate- either wax or hash
- Olive oil

Directions:

Measure 1 cup of olive oil and slow cook in a cooking pot.

Add around 5 grams of THC disengage to plan THC oil. Assuming you are getting ready CBD oil, add around 100 grams of CBD disengage to plan CBD oil.

Stir the combination well for around 5 minutes and eliminate it from

heat. Permit your oil to cool and store in a dull container for later use.

Extracting THC using Butter

Since spread is like oil, it can likewise be utilized as a dissolvable in separating THC and CBD.

Ingredients and Equipment:

- A stainless steel cooking pot
- 1 cup of butter
- 1 cup of finely cut decarboxylated cannabis buds.

Directions:

In the cooking pot, gradually cook the cup of margarine until

completely softened. Add the cup of finely cut decarbed weed buds

and mix gently.

Let your combination of buds and spread stew on low hotness for around 2 hours. This cycle can take up to 8 hours, contingent upon the last oil's favored concentration.

When the blend is very much warmed, eliminate from heat and permit it to cool for around 10 minutes.

Now channel the combination with a fine strainer or cheesecloth to eliminate the leaves.

Now you have a thick, strong oil that will harden back to frame marijuana spread or cannabutter as is famously known.

Cannabutter is similarly just about as significant as CBD and THC oil. Cannabutter can be utilized in preparing a wide range of food. This is the second technique for making cannabutter. There are numerous approaches to getting ready cannabutter, however they all give either CBD or THC strong margarine that can be utilized in cooking.

Cannabis Infusion (How to Make It)

Infuse CBD in Coconut Oil. The most straightforward approach to making THC and CBD oil at home is through an imbuement. The implantation interaction isn't so viable as any of the above techniques, yet it is the most straightforward. Any individual can utilize the mixture technique, even the people who know nothing about cooking.

Unfortunately, to have the option to implant marijuana in your oil expects that you approach new pot buds. In the event that you can't get to new buds, the whole interaction will undoubtedly fizzle. The intensity of the last THC oil is around 3%, while that of CBD oil is around 20%. As may be obvious, imbuement may give you THC and CBD oils, yet they won't be pretty much as strong as expected.

How to make THC and CBD oils through infusion:

- Buy 1 cup of CBD/THC rich fresh cannabis buds.
- Chop your buds into small slices and put them in a dark glass jar.
- Add 1 cup of olive oil to the jar with buds
- Tighten the lid on the jar and place it in the refrigerator.
- Allow your oil and buds to infuse for about 24 hours.
- Remove the jar from the refrigerator and sieve to obtain your CBD or THC oil.
- Refrigerating for 6 hours should be enough to allow your buds to infuse into the oil.

However, assuming you need your oil to be more powerful, permit it to refrigerate for around 48 hours. This oil ought to just be utilized at home and doesn't fulfill the necessary quality guidelines for selling commercially.

Chapter 4:   Where to Buy

Where would I be able to purchase it?

Cannabis isn't sold transparently attributable to its illicit status. You may need to observe a seller who can give you the buds. Prior to getting, you may need to check for quality. The dearest friends are very green and not excessively dry and somewhat tacky all of the time. There is additionally a compacted assortment accessible yet doesn't taste equivalent to the dried ones.

How much does it cost?

The expense of pot relies upon the nature of the plant. The best quality ones will constantly be valued higher than the low and mid-range quality ones. You can deal the cost with your seller assuming you think you are being cheated for it. You can make an inquiry or two to check what the moving costs are, as it will in general change occasionally and season to season.

Why you should grow your cannabis

• Growing clinical pot for own utilization is great

• Investing in the best tent and expanding medium ensures the best results.

• Nutrients ought to be provided to developing marijuana from when they are planted

• How long your weed keeps going relies upon how you store it

• Cannabis plants are excessively impacted by vermin, and they ought to be controlled to stay away from losses

Setting up a developing climate for your pot can be the most ideal choice, regardless of whether you need it for your utilization or business purposes. Dissimilar to previously, when such an action was illicit, you can easily do it now. You ought to, notwithstanding, acclimate yourself first with what maryjane guidelines say in your space of home. Assuming the principles accommodate such self-cultivating exercises, you will actually want to do this sort of work.

Why Grow Your Products?

Well, this is no question a typical inquiry that each weed client frequently asks.

The response is direct, and it should never be a major issue for anybody. Like you develop your carrots or tomatoes at home, developing your own cannabis medication is way less expensive than continuously getting it from a dispensary or the individuals who develop it in your district. Above all, when you do the developing yourself, you give your plant what is required and guarantee that the items you collect are of excellent. Along these lines, it is basic to set up your storeroom to develop at home assuming that you need the best medicine.

Grow Tent

You can get top notch pot assuming you plant it in the right circumstances.

This implies that you ought to direct the developing climate well so you give the plants precisely what they need. For example, they need sufficient light as well as complete dimness around evening time. To accomplish these circumstances, you want a "quality develop tent."

Besides that, here are other smart justifications for why you want a quality develop tent:

• They accompany a waterproof floor consequently simple to clean

• Specially intended to oblige traditional developing equipment

• Smell confirmation as they are set to channel carbon

• They have intelligent dividers to contain light

Expenses

The expense of hardware changes relying upon many variables that incorporate the size, plan, and quality too. Some are modest and go at low costs. Nonetheless, they regularly don't keep going long and probably won't assist you with accomplishing the outcomes you need. Then again, some sell at somewhat greater costs yet have an incredible plan and fabulous quality highlights. We can hence say that there is no particular sum you'll spend. Everything relies upon the plan and the nature of the gear you need to acquire.

Growth Factors

Optimal development factors for pot upgrade solid and best yields from your homestead. Likewise, plants developed under the right circumstances are regularly of top caliber and guarantee receiving all the wellbeing rewards you want. All things considered, here are ideal development factors for cannabis:

• Free and natural air circulation

• Reflective dividers in the tent

• Controlled dampness for quicker growth

• Right temperatures preferably those agreeable to you

• Light that is brilliant yet not excessively bright

The Best Growing Medium

Coco coir is turning into a famous developing medium that is acquiring ubiquity among marijuana ranchers. Specialists likewise suggest utilizing this medium due to the advantages it offers to the plant while making turn out more straightforward for you. Here are motivations to utilize it:

- It is phenomenal for plant roots as it holds dampness and supplements for roots

- Cannabis filled in coco coir is less inclined to be assaulted by pests

- Cannabis filled in coco coir becomes quicker contrasted with that which is filled in soil

- It seems very much like filling in soil however it is soilless

- Coco coir conditions are not positive for garden pests

Pots

More or less, the best pots work with the solid development of plants and keep supplements. Such pots ought to preferably be capable to:

- Allow the roots to take in oxygen

- Find supplements and convey to the developing plant

- Make it simple to oversee soil PH

- Supply dampness at all times

Growing Techniques

The Screen of Green (SCROG) developing procedure is a framework that permits you to get the greatest potential yields from a couple of plants in your tent. As the name recommends, under this framework, weed plants are developed under a screen or lattice. Some specific strains of marijuana, such as the Sativa marijuana strains, grow well using this technique.

Plant Nutrition

Plant nourishment is imperative to be a flourishing marijuana rancher. At each phase of development, plants need supplements to be solid, excellent, and surprisingly delectable for the instance of weed plants. But what kind of nutrients should you provide to your plants? Well, the most important ones are nitrogen, potassium, phosphorus, magnesium, and calcium. Assuming you supply every one of these at the perfect sums, you are guaranteed of the best yields and scrumptious marijuana products.

Caution with Pests

As you develop your weed, you'll experience nuisances and managing some of them can be a troublesome errand. You ought to, consequently, realize the different vermin control strategies that you can use to keep them under control. On the off chance that you neglect to do that, you allow them an opportunity to obliterate your plants and furthermore influence the nature of the items you'll develop. Assuming you choose to utilize synthetics to control them, guarantee that you are acquainted with the rules and conceivable secondary effects for your plants.

Marijuana Supply

Good things typically reach a conclusion, and that is the case too for the maryjane supply. Albeit many see it as a supernatural plant, it also has an expiry date when it becomes pointless in the event that it's not used on schedule. Presently, the central issue is, when does weed terminate? Indeed, there is no particular solution to this inquiry as it relies upon many elements. All the more explicitly, it relies upon how you store it and the structure it is handled in the wake of collecting it.

Electricity Cost

If you choose to develop weed inside, you should utilize power and bring about some expense. The expense relies upon numerous realities, including the quantity of tents or space you are lighting. To illustrate what's in store, the normal power cost each month for CFLs is $27/month. Then again, the normal power cost each month for 100WLED is between $10 and $20.

Chapter 5:   Quick History of Cannabis

History of Cannabis

Cannabis, or all the more prevalently known as weed, has been around for millennia. Antiquated civic establishments, similar to the Ancient Greeks and the Assyrians, have archived this plant for clinical employments. Even prehistoric civilizations dating back to 12,000 years ago are believed to have used marijuana. Consumed marijuana seeds dated to be from around 3,000 BC were found in Siberia. Burial places of aristocrats tracing all the way back to 2500 BC in China's Xinjiang region were found to contain a lot of preserved marijuana.

The most established recorded utilization of pot was in 2727 BC from the Chinese Emperor Shen Nung. Pot from China was accepted to have spread to South Asia. Whenever the Aryans attacked South Asia, they carried pot with them to India.

The plant arrived in the Middle East then spread to Ukraine, South Russia, and eventually to Europe. Germanic clans were accepted to have carried marijuana to Europe. There were hints of marijuana seeds found in old Viking ships. The plant showed up in Britain at some point during the fifth century.

Cannabis tracked down its direction to the United States during the beginning of the twentieth century. It showed up in the US through Mexico. It was brought by foreigners going to the US to get away from the Mexican Revolution during the mid 1900s.

Sativa is generally acknowledged as the main weed species. The French distinguished the Indica strain. A third strain, Ruderalis, was distinguished in 1924 by a Russian botanist. This third strain isn't broadly developed and utilized today, similar to the next two.

Statistics on Cannabis Use

Surprisingly, the UN has information on which nations smoke the most weed every year. As per the UN Office on Drugs and crime:

10% of Jamaica's populace appreciate cannabis. The Jamaican government has as of late decriminalized the plant.

10% of Australians use pot, regardless of being illicit in the country.

More than 10% of the populace in Spain partake in weed. Most partake in maryjane in excess of 800 private marijuana clubs in the country where enrollment is required. However, a deal is illicit. Residents are not punished for secretly developing or consuming cannabis.

Marijuana is actually illicit in The Netherlands, yet specialists practice capacity to bear low-level utilization. Cafés in Amsterdam much proposition pot however don't straightforwardly promote it. Just occupants with a "wiretaps card" are permitted in these "cafés." However, vacationers can without much of a stretch get into these shops for some cannabis.

Medical pot use is legitimate in Canada. The Cannabis Act passed in 2018 made Canada the subsequent nation (first was Uruguay) to legitimize sporting weed. Notwithstanding, the law has many arrangements that safeguard the adolescent and lawbreakers from profiting from the legalization.

14% of the populace in Nigeria appreciate marijuana, despite the fact that it is unlawful in the country.

14% of the populace in Italy consume pot. Individual use is legitimate in the nation however illicit to develop and sell.

18.3% of Iceland's populace partakes in maryjane, where it is illegal.

In the U.S., ten states and the District of Columbia have legitimized cannabis for sporting use. Another 21 states have passed wide regulations that permit the clinical utilization of marijuana.

The plant was added to Western medication rehearses By W.B. O'Shaughnessy in 1839. He was a specialist who found out with regards to marijuana's clinical properties when he worked for the British East India Company in India. Marijuana was advanced as a soothing, antispasmodic, anticonvulsant, pain relieving, and calming specialist. It was acknowledged as a clinical plant. The US Treasury Department even forced the Marihuana Tax Act in 1937. The law forced a $1 demand for every ounce of clinical marijuana use and $100 demand for non-clinical use.

The American Medical Association reliably went against the utilization of pot. Specialists are expected to pay extraordinary duties each time they recommend pot. They likewise need a request structure when they are to get pot. They likewise need to keep a record enumerating their expert pot use.

The gathering was sure that the utilization of pot for clinical purposes needed abundant logical evidence. Marijuana was before long eliminated from US pharmacopeia in 1942 because of the persevering worries over its adverse consequence on wellbeing. US

Congress in 1951 passed the Boggs Act. This recorded weed under opiate drugs. Concerns continued until in 1970, and weed was named a Schedule 1 medication upon the section of the Controlled Substances Act.
Schedule 1 method it doesn't have any perceived or acknowledged clinical use. This class included LSD, heroin, methaqualone, and mescaline.

On the other hand, there was additionally a determined work to get weed perceived for its clinical employments. In 1978, the US government laid out the Compassionate Use Investigational New Drug program. It permitted the case-to-case premise utilization of weed for certain patients.

In the succeeding years, states began passing regulations that permitted marijuana use in shifting degrees. These states have permitted pot use notwithstanding government regulations holding its stand that maryjane is illegal.

Some states have permitted the full utilization of pot, both sporting and clinical. Some permitted development, deal, and use for diversion and clinical. Some main permitted clinical use and just with a clinical card. Some took into account utilize yet not development. A few states just permitted CBD yet not the entire plant for clinical use.

The greatest road obstruction and wellspring of discussion is whether or not pot has clinical use. Assuming there are any health advantages, do these advantages offset the potential mischief it causes?

Chapter 6:   CBD Proper Intake

Quality of CBD Oil

CBD iS a quickly developing industry. The new blast in utilization implies that many organizations are attempting to benefit from selling CBD as they can. There is a high likelihood that not every one of them are worried about placing the best and best item available. The CBD oil is filling in fame, and many organizations are putting different unstandardized items out there. The customers are left confounded with regards to the unwavering quality of the item. Here are a portion of the manners in which you can distinguish quality CBD oil. Additionally, look at what organizations got the official endorsement by the U.S. Hemp Authority.

Ingredients

A decent quality CBD oil doesn't have more than a few fixings in it. CBD doesn't function admirably in the event that it is consumed absolutely all alone. It appears as though table salt when it is in 100% unadulterated structure newly extricated from the plant. It should be mixed with oil to work actually. By stirring up with oil, the human body can ingest it and process promptly. The unadulterated CBD is assimilated lesser than the one injected with a transporter oil. A top notch transporter oil is the most pivotal fixing to any oral cannabidiol. A decent quality item will have 250-1,000 mg for every liquid ounce of CBD. CBD amount in an item might change, so make certain to pay special attention to CBD's sum prior to buying it. Hemp seed oil, olive oil, MCT oil, and coconut oil make up great transporter oil.
However, since hemp seed oil comes from a similar plant as the CBD comes from, it is likely the one that works the best.

Manufacturing

Different CBD brands have different extraction strategies. A few strategies that organizations utilize might be modest ones, and they can leave behind hints of harmful solvents.

The CO2 extraction strategy is costly and more intricate than different ones. This strategy produces CBD oil that has held its virtue all through the extraction cycle.

A few organizations additionally use natural, drug grade ethanol to remove CBD. The utilization of ethanol eliminates the poisons and deposits that are abandoned from the hemp plant. This extraction technique has the best return of cannabinoids when contrasted with different cycles. It is likewise viewed as one of the most secure method for extraction.

So, before you buy any CBD oil, do a little research on their creation strategy. You can track down this data on their site. The ones that are created from C02 or ethanol strategies are recommended.

The Source of CBD

The hemp plant is known to be a hyper-collector. This implies it ingests everything without exception that exists in the dirt. Assuming the ground in which hemp developed is ripe, the plant will be of good quality. Great quality plant implies great quality CBD oil.

If the ground where hemp plant was created is defiled with weighty metals, then, at that point, the CBD oil delivered from it will have similar weighty metals in them too. This makes it dangerous for people to consume.

CBD oil has a danger of fostering an awful standing since certain makers couldn't care less with regards to the nature of the hemp that they use. The outcome is that the item they produce may be loaded down with poisonous weighty metals.

Try to utilize items produced using US-developed hemp. The state branch of horticulture confirms the ranchers, so it is proposed that to know the nature of CBD oil, research where they source their hemp from. This data should be accessible on the site of the retailer or the manufacturer.

Amount of THC in the CBD oil.

THC is answerable for the psychotropic impacts brought about by the admission of maryjane or farming hemp. Hemp is utilized over maryjane for the creation of CBD oil since it contains lower levels of THC. The THC sum in hemp is pitiful, yet it is still there and can cause hallucinogenic impacts on the off chance that it isn't handled really. CBD oil is fabricated from countless hemp plants. Assuming the plant's handling is done inadequately, the created CBD oil might have significantly more THC than the suggested level.

It is proposed that how much THC in CBD oil ought not be more than 0.3 percent. You can check for this data on the mark of the product.

Isolates or full spectrum

Good CBD oil is made from utilizing the entire plant. This guarantees that the oil contains CBD and every one of the essential and optional parts of the hemp plant. These different parts are flavonoids, terpenes, and other cannabinoids. They raise the effectivity of CBD more than if it is utilized simply on its own.

CBD segregates contain just the Cannabidiol compound. Detaches have no THC in them, which is extraordinary for kids, or individuals who are landing tried for their positions and don't have any desire to chance follow measures of THC appearing in their results.

You can actually take a look at the names on the item. It will let you know if the producer utilized the entire plant or full spectrum.

Third-party test results

The brand that produces great CBD generally gives outsider outcomes to their clients. The tests from autonomous labs will guarantee the nature of the CBD oil that you are buying. These tests will fulfill the purchasers about item unwavering quality and whether or not every one of the cases they made are valid. Essential things to search for are low THC, high amount of CBD, and absence of poisons and impurities.

A decent and trustworthy brand will continuously make the new lab results accessible for the clients. They might be on the site or in the bundling of the item. On the off chance that you can't observe the experimental outcomes, try to reach them for it. Phenomenal client assistance is a sign 100% of the time of a decent product.

The authorize labs to ISO/IEC 17025:2017 test CBD to ensure that

It is liberated from the following:

- Residual harmful solvents
- Fungus or bacteria
- Pesticides
- Heavy metals
- Any other foreign material

The Dosage of CBD Oil

You should accurately observe the best measurements for YOUR requirements. Continuously start exceptionally low. For instance, assuming you utilize a 500 mg oil, I would begin with 3 - 5 drops, two times each day. Take notes on how you feel. Then slowly increase the dosage until you feel better. Assuming you begin to feel more awful, after an increment, bring down the measurement again.

If you start with an excess of CBD, in uncommon cases, it could cause Flu-like indications, tantamount to the Keto-Flu, when you start with Keto.

That's the reason SLOWER is BETTER!

The normal CBD portion can be somewhere close to 10 mg and 50 mg taken at one to three times each day. Higher dosages might be utilized to control torment. They are endured by our bodies quite well. Various items have various centralizations of CBD. That is one reason that some will see consequences for the lower-portion range while others might require taking more to see the equivalent effects.

How Do You Take CBD Oils?

In food

Adding CBD oil to your food makes it simpler to take in. You can make your edibles or buy premade food varieties that are implanted with CBD. Assuming you make the supper yourself, you need to deal with how much CBD oil to place in your food and the amount you eat. Edibles require two to four hours to take effect.

Some experts of this technique are that out of any remaining utilization strategies, and it has the most durable impact. You have various choices to look over on how you need to consume the CBD. You can evaluate new shakes, food plans, etc.

Some cons are that it can consume most of the day to kick in, as long as four hours. You additionally need to take care to discover the right portion. This is particularly obvious assuming you purchase food or beverages that case to have CBD in it. Typically, you simply don't know.

Vaping

You can likewise vape CBD oil with a vaporizer pen. Vaping is an option in contrast to smoking. It grants the greatest conceivable impact without being impeding to your throat or lungs. Everything however we don't have the foggiest idea about the drawn out impacts on vaping yet.

Some geniuses of this technique are that it guarantees ideal impact because of high focus. You can undoubtedly screen how much portion you take.

Some cons of this technique are that high focus may not be the thing you are searching for. It additionally expects you to buy a few adornments (e.g., a vape pen).

Capsules

CBD can be ingested by means of containers or in powder structure. It goes through the gastrointestinal system and afterward gets consumed in the circulation system. Then, at that point, by blood, it can go all through your whole body.

Some geniuses of this technique: This is the most ideal way to search for long haul supplementation. It can likewise assist you with controlling the portion of CBD oil.

A con connected with this technique: It invests in some opportunity for CBD to arrive at its targets.

Sublingually

CBD oil colors are additionally accessible, and they come in bottles that seem as though eye drops. You can put a couple of drops under your tongue and hold them in there for roughly thirty seconds. A few benefits of this technique are that it is circumspect and simple to utilize. Controlling your measurement is easy.

This strategy works the quickest, so assuming that you really want a prompt method for disposing of pressure or torment, you should accept the CBD oil under your tongue. The impacts will probably last a couple hours.

Chapter 7:   Marijuana Cookies and Bars Recipes

1. Cannabutter Cookie

- ¾ cup
- cannabutter 1 cup
- brown sugar 1
  egg
- 1 teaspoon
- vanilla 2 ½ cups
  flour
- ½ teaspoon baking powder
- 1 teaspoon salt

PREPARATION: 10-15 MINUTES | COOKING: 10 MINUTES | SERVINGS: 14-16

Directions:

1. In a huge bowl, beat the spread until it is fluffy.
2. Add the sugar, egg, and vanilla. Blend well.
3. In an alternate bowl, blend the flour, baking powder, and salt.
4. Add it to the margarine combination, and blend the fixings to frame a delicate dough.
5. Divide the batter into equal parts, smooth it, and envelop the plates by saran wrap. Refrigerate for 60-90 minutes.
6. Line a treat sheet with material paper and preheat the broiler to 375°F.
7. Take it out and move every 50% of the mixture to a ¼-inch thickness.
8. Cut out round treat shapes utilizing a cutout. Improve the excess batter until it is all used.
9. Place the treats 1 inch separated on the pre-arranged treat sheet.
10. Bake for 10 minutes.
11. Serve warm!

Nutrition: Calories: 110 Cal - Fat: 0.5 g - Carbs: 24 g - Fiber: 0.7 g - Protein: 2.4 g

2. Orange Canna Cookie

Ingredients:

- ½ cup cannabutter
- ⅔ Cup sugar
- 1 tablespoon orange zest
- 1 teaspoon orange juice
- 1 egg
- ½ teaspoon baking soda
- 1 ¼ cups flour
- Dash of salt
- 1 tablespoons poppy seeds

PREPARATION: 15 MINUTES | COOKING: 8-10 MINUTES | SERVINGS: 36

Directions:

1. Preheat the broiler to 350°F.
2. In a medium-sized bowl, beat the cannabutter and sugar until fluffy.
3. Add the orange zing, squeeze, and egg; blend well.
4. In a different bowl, join the baking pop, flour, and salt.
5. Add the dry fixings to the egg combination and blend to consolidate well.
6. Add the poppy seeds.
7. Drop spoonfuls of the mixture on the treat sheets, leaving 2 crawls between each.
8. Bake for around 10-12 minutes.
9. Remove from the hotness and let them cool down for a couple minutes.

10.   Serve warm!

Nutrition: Calories: 33 Cal - Fat: 0.3 g - Carbs: 70 g - Fiber: 2.2 g - Protein: 0.6 g

3.Italian Espresso Brownies

Ingredients:

- 4 ounces bittersweet
- chocolate 3 tablespoons
- unsalted butter 1 ½ cups
  white sugar
- ½ cup of cane sugar
- 2 tablespoons cannabutter
- 1 teaspoon vanilla
- Pinch of salt
- 3 eggs
- 1 cup all-purpose flour
- 1 teaspoon ground Italian espresso beans

PREPARATION: 15-20 MINUTES | COOKING: 40 MINUTES | SERVINGS: 16

Directions:

1. Preheat the stove to 350°F.
2. Lightly oil a 9x13 brownie dish, and afterward line it with aluminum foil.
3. Melt the chocolate in a medium pot over medium-low heat.
4. Add the normal spread, white sugar, and stick sugar.
5. Thoroughly whisk the combination to liquefy all the sugar completely.
6. Add the cannabutter, vanilla, salt, and eggs. Race for two minutes.

7. Add the flour and coffee, and consolidate well with the chocolate mixture.

8. Spread the player into the pan.

9. Bake for around 40 minutes.

10. Enjoy the brownies solo, or with your favorite hot coffee.

4. Canna Chocolate Brownie

Ingredients:

- ¼ cup butter
- ¼ cup cannabutter
- 1 cup of chocolate chips
- ¾ cup self-rising
- flour 1 ½ teaspoons
- vanilla 1 cup sugar
- 2 eggs

PREPARATION: 10 MINUTES | COOKING: 30 MINUTES | SERVINGS: 12-14

Directions:

1. Preheat the stove to 350°F and daintily oil a 9-inch square baking pan.

2. Melt the margarine, cannabutter, and chocolate contributes an enormous saucepan.

3. Remove the container from the hotness and add the excess fixings; join well.

4. Spread the hitter in the baking pan.

5. Bake for a large portion of an hour.

6. Take them out and allow them to chill off for a couple minutes.

7. Cut, and serve warm!

5.Nutritious Oatmeal Bar

Ingredients:

- 1 teaspoon baking soda
- ⅔ Cup cannabutter, melted
- ⅔ Cup honey
- 1 cup all-purpose flour
- 2 teaspoons vanilla extract
- ⅓ Cup brown sugar
- 5 cups oatmeal
- 2 cups mixture of raisins, coconut flakes, pecans, walnuts, and chocolate chips

PREPARATION: 10 MINUTES | COOKING: 30 MINUTES | SERVINGS: 8-10

Directions:

1. Preheat the broiler to 325°F.
2. Grease a 9x13 baking dish with cooking spray.
3. Thoroughly blend every one of the fixings in a huge bowl.
4. Pour the combination into the pre-arranged baking skillet, and press it delicately to an even thickness.
5. Bake for 25-30 minutes, until it is a light brilliant color.
6. Cool for 30 minutes.
7. Cut into pieces and serve!

6. Peanut Butter Canna Cookies

Ingredients:

- ½ cup cannabutter
- ½ cup peanut butter
- 1 ¼ cups flour, divided
- 1 egg
- 1 ½ cups white sugar, divided
- ½ cup brown sugar
- ½ teaspoon baking powder
- ½ teaspoon baking soda
- 1 teaspoon vanilla

PREPARATION: 15-20 MINUTES | COOKING: 8-10 MINUTES | SERVINGS: 24

   extract

Directions:

1. Preheat a stove to 350 F.
2. Heat the cannabutter for 30-40 seconds in a microwave until it melts.
3. Mix the liquefied cannabutter and nut butter.
4. Add ¾ cup of the flour, the egg, and 1 cup of the white sugar, the earthy colored sugar, baking powder, baking pop, and vanilla extract.
5. Mix completely, and afterward blend in the leftover flour.
6. Pour the leftover ½ cup of white sugar into a little bowl.
7. Form the batter into 1-inch balls, and roll the balls in the sugar to coat.
8. Place the covered balls on a baking sheet.

9. Bake for 10 minutes.

10. Serve warm with a glass of milk.

Nutrition: Calories: 117 Cal - Fat: 3 g - Carbs: 21 g - Fiber: 5.6 g - Protein: 2.5 g

7. Cranberry Canna Bars

Ingredients:

For the crust:

- ¾ cups white sugar
- 1 ½ cups all-purpose flour
- ¼ teaspoon salt
- ¾ cup cannabutter

For the topping:

- 1 cup sweetened dried cranberries
- 2 cups sweetened flaked coconut
- ¾ cups brown sugar, packed
- 1 ½ teaspoons vanilla
- 3 eggs, beaten

PREPARATION: 25 MINUTES | COOKING: 40 MINUTES | SERVINGS: 36

Directions:

1. Preheat the broiler to 350°F.
2. In a medium-sized bowl, consolidate the white sugar, earthy colored sugar, flour, and salt.
3. Add the cannabutter and utilizing clean hands, rub it into the flour and sugar to make a brittle mixture.
4. Press the blend into the lower part of a 9x13 baking pan.
5. Bake for a couple of moments, until the edges are softly golden.

6. Mix every one of the fixing fixings in a huge bowl and pour it over the

   hull. Spread it out evenly.

7. Bake for 22-25 minutes until the custard is set and the edges are

   lightly golden.

8. Canna Roasted Almond Cookies

Ingredients:

- 1 cup cannabutter, softened
- ¼ cup sugar
- 1 teaspoon pure vanilla
- extract 2 cups all-purpose
  flour
- ½ cup roasted almonds, finely chopped
- ¼ teaspoon salt
- 2 tablespoons cornstarch
- 1 cup powdered sugar (for coating purpose)

PREPARATION: 12-15 MINUTES | COOKING: 30 MINUTES | SERVINGS: 26

Directions:

1. In a huge bowl, blend the cannabutter with the sugar until it
   is creamy.
2. Add the vanilla concentrate, flour, broiled almonds,
   salt, and cornstarch.
3. Thoroughly blend the ingredients.
4. Cover the bowl with foil, and refrigerate for 60-90 minutes.
5. Preheat the broiler to 325°F.

6. Form the batter into 1-inch balls and orchestrate them on a baking sheet.

7. Bake for 20-25 minutes.

8. Put the powdered sugar in a bowl.

9. Coat the treat balls with powdered sugar.

10. Cool on a rack fixed with material paper.

11. Serve warm!

9. Cocoa Canna-Brownies

Ingredients:

- 2/3 cup of pecan or walnut pieces
- 1/2 cup of flour, all-purpose
- 2 eggs, large
- 1/2 tbsp. of vanilla, pure
- 1/4 tsp. of salt, kosher
- 3/4 cup of unsweetened cocoa powder
- 1 & 1/4 cups of sugar, granulated
- 10 tbsp. of cannabis butter

PREPARATION: 20 MINUTES | COOKING: 40 MINUTES | SERVINGS: 25

Directions:

1. Line sides and lower part of 8" square baking skillet. Leave the baking paper looming over on two sides.

2. Set a hotness resistant, medium-sized bowl in a huge skillet with water. Bring to stew. Dissolve marijuana margarine. Add the salt, sugar, and cocoa. Blend well.

3. Stir as the dish cooks. The combination should be hot and

smooth. Eliminate bowl from the skillet and permit it to cool
a bit.

4. Stir in vanilla. Add eggs, in a steady progression, mixing
    energetically after each egg.

5. When the player is all around mixed, gleaming and thick, include
    flour. Mix to consolidate well. Beat for 40 additional strokes. Mix
    in nuts.

6. Spread blend in the baking skillet. Prepare for 20-30 minutes at
    325F. Eliminate. Permit cooling on wire rack completely.

7. Use the baking paper to transfer the brownies to cutting board.
    Slice into 25 individual pieces. Serve.

Nutrition: Calories: 71 Cal - Carbs: 15 g - Fat: 13 g - Protein: 1 g - Fiber: 2.5 g

10. Magic Canna Cookies

Ingredients:

- 1 cup of chocolate chips, milk
- 1 cup of coconut, shredded
- 1 can of milk, condensed
- 1 cup of crumbs, graham cracker
- 1 cup of melted cannabis butter

PREPARATION: 10 MINUTES | COOKING: 20 MINUTES | SERVINGS: 4-6

Directions:

1. Preheat the stove to 350F.

2. Melt the pot spread. Fill 13x9" baking dish.

3. Then sprinkle the graham wafer morsels on top.

4. Press to frame the crust.

5. Sprinkle chocolate chips and coconut over the graham saltine crust.

6. Pour the dense milk over mixture.

7. Bake for 20-25 minutes. Cut into bars.

8. Serve.

11. Orange Poppy Seed Cookies

Ingredients:

- 1/2 tsp. of baking
- soda 1 tbsp. of orange
- zest 1 tsp. orange juice
- 1 tbsp. of poppy
- seeds 1/2 cup of
- cannabutter 2/3 cup of sugar
- 1 1/4 cup of flour
- 1 egg
- Dash of salt

Directions:

1. Set the broiler to 350°F for preheating.

2. Whisk the sugar and cannabutter together for around 2 minutes. This will leave a light player, moderately fluffy.

3. Add the orange zing, the squeezed orange, and the egg, making a

point to blend every one for best outcomes thoroughly.

4. Take another bowl and filter the baking pop, salt, and flour together.

5. Add the filtered blend to the first hitter, and blend simply to the point of seeing them consolidated prior to collapsing in the poppy seeds. Tip: For chewier treats, line the treat sheets prior to baking. Parchment

    paper works best!

6. The blend is presently fit to be set onto the treat sheets. Take a teaspoon and package out the pieces, trying to leave even spaces between each cookie.

7. Place in the oven and bake for about 10-12 minutes, the cookies are ultimately done when the edges are golden. Remove from the heat, let them cool down, and enjoy!

Nutrition: Calories: 276 Cal - Fat: 14 g - Protein: 26 g - Carbs: 45 g

12. Canna Oatmeal Cookies

Ingredients:

- 1 cup of chopped
- pecans 2 cups of oats, rolled
- 1 ½ cups of raisins
- 1/2 tsp. of baking soda
- 2 cups of flour, whole-
- wheat 1 tbsp. of cinnamon,
- ground 1 tbsp. of nutmeg, ground

- 2 tsp. of vanilla extract,

- pure 2 cups of sugar, raw

- 3/4 cup of cannabis

- butter 2 eggs, large

- 2 tbsp. of water,

- filtered 1 tsp. of sea

salt

PREPARATION: 15 MINUTES | COOKING: 30 | SERVINGS: 2-3 DOZEN COOKIES

Directions:

1. Preheat the stove to 350F.
2. Cream vanilla, sugar, marijuana spread and eggs together in a bowl.
3. Combine salt, baking pop, flour and flavors into the cream mixture.
4. Add walnuts, oats, raisins and water. Blend well.
5. Chill the treat batter in ice chest for 15-20 minutes.
6. Spoon 1-inch bundles of mixture onto a lined treat sheet.
7. Bake at 350F for 12-18 minutes. Tops ought to turn out to be marginally browned.
8. Cool and serve.

Nutrition: Calories: 66 Cal - Carbs: 14 g - Fat: 1.3 g - Protein: 1.1 g - Fiber: 2.2 g

Chapter 8:   Cannabis Muffin Recipes

13. Blueberry Cannabis Muffins

Ingredients:

- Muffin baking tin
- Paper cupcake liners
- 1 ½ cups all-purpose flour
- ¾ cup of white sugar
- ½ teaspoon of salt
- 2 teaspoons of baking powder
- ½ cup Canna oil
- 1 egg
- ⅓ Cup of Canna milk
- 1 cup of fresh blueberries
- ½ cup of white sugar
- ⅓ Cup of all-purpose flour

Directions:

1. Preheat the stove to 400 degrees.
2. Line biscuit cups with paper liners.
3. Combine flour, sugar, salt and baking powder.
4. Put to the side. Place Canna oil in a 1-cup estimating cup and add the egg and enough Canna milk to fill the cup.
5. Add to the flour combination and stir.
6. Fold blueberries into the batter.
7. Fill the biscuit cups up and sprinkle each cup with ground cinnamon.
8. Bake in the preheated stove for 20 to 25 minutes.

14. Quinoa Corn Cannabis Muffins

Ingredients:

- 1 cup of cooked or ½ cup of raw quinoa
- ½ cup grilled or cooked corn (cut the cob)
- 1 cup whole-wheat pastry flour (or favorite canna flour)
- 1 cup quinoa flour (look in the bulk section at the health food store)
- ¼ teaspoon of salt
- 1 teaspoon of baking soda
- ½ cup packaged light brown sugar (or low impact favorite sweetener)
- 1 egg
- ¼ cup of cannabis butter, melted
- 1 ¼ cup of yogurt
- 1 teaspoon of vanilla extract

PREPARATION: 21 MINUTES | COOKING: 35 MINUTES | SERVINGS: 8

Directions:

1. First, preheat Your broiler to 375° and oil your biscuit tin. You can utilize a small scale biscuit tin or a standard biscuit tin, yet I incline toward a smaller than usual biscuit tin since it is more straightforward to portion your food.

2. If you really want to cook your quinoa, put it in a pot with 1 cup of water and heat to the point of boiling. Cover the skillet and decrease the hotness to low. You realize it is prepared when all the water is retained and the microbe, or 'tail', emerges from the grain. Cushion with a fork, eliminate from hotness and pass on covered until prepared to use.

3. To make the biscuit player, join the two sorts of flour, salt, baking

pop, and sugar in a blending bowl. Utilize one more bowl to blend the egg, dissolved pot margarine, yogurt and vanilla.

4. Stir the wet fixings into the dry fixings and add the cooked quinoa and corn. Make a point to scratch the base and sides of the bowl and ensure all the flour is retained. Spoon the hitter into the biscuit tin and prepare for 25 minutes utilizing standard size tins and 15 minutes utilizing a smaller than normal biscuit tin.

5. Muffins are golden brown and feel firm when they are done baking.

Nutrition: Calories: 184 Cal - Carbs: 26 g - Fat: 3.2 g - Protein: 2.7 g

15. Bacon & Egg Muffins

Ingredients:

- 4 flour tortillas
- 4 teaspoons cannabutter, melted
- 1 cup of grated cheddar cheese
- 4 strips of bacon, cooked and chopped
- 4 large eggs, at room temperature
- Salt and black pepper

PREPARATION: 20 MINUTES | COOKING: 30 MINUTES | SERVINGS: 4

Directions:

1. Preheat the stove to 340 ° F.
2. Press the flour tortillas in 4 cups in a standard biscuit dish. Brush within the tortilla cups with the cannabutter.
3. Spread 3/4 cup of cheddar over the tortilla cups. Get done with the cleaved bacon. Cautiously break an egg into every tortilla cup.

Spread uniformly over the excess cheddar. Sprinkle with salt and dark pepper.

4. Bake until the eggs have solidified, around 10 minutes. Serve immediately.

5. Chef's Note: If the tortillas appear to be weak, heat them in the microwave for 10 seconds to mellow them. To carry the eggs to room temperature, place them in a bowl of tepid water for 20 minutes.

Nutrition: Calories: 176 Cal - Carbs: 36 g - Protein: 2.8 g - Sodium: 376 mg

16. Cannabis Chia Seed and Berry Muffins

Ingredients:

- 1½ cups all-purpose flour
- 1 large egg
- ½ cup granulated sugar
- ¾ cup of non-fat Greek yogurt
- ¼ cup of liquid Canna Oil
- 2 tablespoons of honey
- 1½ teaspoons of baking powder
- ¾ teaspoon of grated lemon zest
- ¼ teaspoon of pure vanilla extract
- ¼ teaspoon of baking soda
- ¼ teaspoon of salt
- 1/8 teaspoon of ground cinnamon
- 1 1/3 cups fresh or frozen berries we used equal parts blueberries, raspberries and cranberries
- 2 tablespoons of chia seeds

Directions:

1. Preheat your broiler to 375 degrees. Pipe a small biscuit tin with cooking splash and set aside.

2. In a medium bowl, beat the egg and sugar for about a minute.

3. Add the yogurt, Canna Oil, honey, vanilla concentrate, cinnamon, and
lemon zing and beat to combine.

4. In a different blending bowl, beat the flour, baking powder, baking powder and salt together until there are no lumps.

5. Pour the wet fixings over the dry ingredients.

6. Mix until recently consolidated. Be mindful so as not to over blend. A too blended hitter makes thick biscuits. The player will be very thick, practically like treat dough.

7. Carefully overlay in the berries and chia seeds.

8. Spoon full tablespoons of hitter into the pre-arranged biscuit tin. You ought to have sufficient player for around 20 small scale muffins.

9. Bake for 15-17 minutes until the top is brilliant brown and a toothpick embedded into the focal point of the biscuits comes out clean.

10. Let the muffins cool in the tin for about 10 minutes, then transfer them to a plate or rack to cool completely.

Nutrition: Calories: 167 Cal - Carbs: 32g - Fat: 4.2 g - Protein: 2.6 g

17. Marmalade Muffins

Ingredients:

- 1 cup plain flour
- 1/4 cup brown sugar
- 1 large egg
- 2/3 cup orange juice
- 1/2 cup yogurt
- 1 tsp. Baking powder
- 1/2 tsp. Baking soda
- 1/2 tsp. Salt
- 1 tsp. Grated orange zest
- 1/2 tsp. Vanilla extract
- 1 stick melted cannabis-infused butter
- 9 tsp. Marmalade

PREPARATION: 20 MINUTES | COOKING: 45 MINUTES | SERVINGS: 9

Directions:

1. Preheat broiler to 375 F. Oil 9 biscuit tin wells or line with paper cups.

2. In an enormous bowl, whisk together the flour, sugar, baking powder, baking pop, orange zing, vanilla and salt.

3. In a different bowl, whisk together the egg, yogurt, margarine and squeezed orange Combine with dry blend; don't over-mix.

4. Spoon 1 tbsp of the mixture into each muffin case, top with 1 tsp. of marmalade, then cover with the remaining muffin mix. Bake for 15-18 minutes or until tops start to brown and a toothpick inserted into a muffin comes out clean. Remove from the oven, transfer to a

Nutrition: Calories: 107 Cal - Carbs: 26g - Fat: 1.4 g - Protein: 2 g - Sodium: 123 mg

wire rack and leave to cool.

18. Healthy Cannabis Muffins

Ingredients:

- 1 cup whole wheat flour
- 1 cup plain flour
- 1/4 cup brown sugar
- 3 large eggs
- 1 tsp. baking powder
- 1 tsp. baking soda
- 1 tsp. salt
- 1/2 tsp. vanilla extract
- 1 cup yogurt
- 1 cup cannabis-infused olive
- oil 1 cup mashed banana
- 1/2 cup pureed apples
- 2 tbsp. mixed seeds (pumpkin, sunflower and flaxseed)

PREPARATION: 15 MINUTES | COOKING: 25 MINUTES | SERVINGS: 10

Directions:

1. Preheat broiler to 375 F. Oil 12 biscuit tin wells or line with paper cups.
2. In a huge bowl, whisk together the flour, sugar, baking powder, baking pop, vanilla and salt.
3. In a different bowl, whisk together the eggs, yogurt, olive oil, crushed banana and apple puree. Join with dry combination; don't over-mix.

4. Spoon batter into prepared muffin tin. Sprinkle the muffins with the seeds. Bake for 15-18 minutes or until tops start to brown and a toothpick inserted into a muffin comes out clean. Remove from the oven, transfer to a wire rack and leave to cool.

Nutrition: Calories: 187 Cal - Carbs: 28 g - Fat: 2.3 g - Protein: 4 g - Sodium: 1.3 mg

19. Blueberry Oats Muffins

Ingredients:

- 1 cup flour
- ½ cup quick oats
- ¼ cup sugar
- 2 teaspoons baking powder
- ½ teaspoon
- salt 1 egg
- ¾ cup milk
- ¼ cup cannabutter
- ¾ cup blueberries

PREPARATION: 10 MINUTES | COOKING: 25 MINUTES | SERVINGS: 10-12 MUFFINS

Directions:

1. Preheat the broiler to 400°F.
2. Line 12 biscuit tins with paper liners.
3. In an enormous blending bowl, consolidate the flour, oats, sugar, baking powder, and salt.
4. Create an opening in the focal point of the dry fixings and set the bowl aside.
5. In a little bowl, blend the egg, milk, and cannabutter.

6. Pour the wet fixings into the indent in the dry fixings, and mix until they are simply combined.

7. Add the blueberries and overlap them into the batter.

8. Fill the biscuit cups around 3/4 full.

9. Bake for 20-25 minutes.

Nutrition: Calories: 102 Cal - Carbs: 20 g - Fat: 1.2 g - Protein: 3 g - Sodium: 133 mg

20. Banana Cannabis Muffins

Ingredients:

- ½ cup vegetable oil
- 6 grams of cannabis, ground
- 1 ½ cups plus 2 tablespoons all-purpose flour, divided
- 1 teaspoon baking powder
- 1 teaspoon baking soda
- ½ teaspoon
- salt 1 egg,

  beaten
- 3 bananas, mashed
- ¾ cup white sugar
- ⅓ Cup brown sugar
- ⅛ Teaspoon cinnamon, ground
- 1 tablespoon butter, unsalted

PREPARATION: 15 MINUTES | COOKING: 20 MINUTES | SERVINGS: 18-20 MUFFINS

Directions:

1. Warm the oil in a pan, and add the cannabis.

2. Heat for around 15-20 minutes over medium hotness. Set it aside.

3. Strain the combination through a piece of cheesecloth or metal sifter, pressing delicately to remove the oil.

4. Preheat the broiler to 375°F, and line the biscuit cups with biscuit papers.

5. In a huge blending bowl, consolidate 1 ½ cups of flour, baking powder,
baking pop, and salt.

6. In a different bowl, join the egg, bananas, white sugar, and the extricated oil. Blend well.

7. Add the banana combination to the flour combination, and blend until the hitter moistens.

8. Fill the lined biscuit cups around 66% full with the batter.

9. In a little blending bowl, join the earthy colored sugar, cinnamon, and the excess 2 tablespoons of universally handy flour. Add the spread and blend again until crumbly.

10. Top the biscuits with this mixture.

11. Bake for around 18-20 minutes. Serve warm!

Nutrition: Calories: 147 Cal - Carbs: 22 g - Fat: 6.4 g - Protein: 1.5 g - Sodium: 130 mg

21. Five-Ingredient Banana Muffins

Ingredients:

- 3 very ripe bananas
- 3 large eggs
- ¾ cup peanut butter
- ¼ cup canna-oil (here)
- ¾ teaspoon baking powder

PREPARATION: 10 MINUTES | COOKING: 25 MINUTES | SERVINGS: 1 MUFFIN

Directions:

1. Preheat the stove to 340°F.
2. In a food processor, join the bananas, eggs, peanut butter, canna-oil, and baking powder. Process for 1 to 2 minutes until smooth.
3. Pour the blend into a nonstick, or lubed, biscuit pan.
4. Bake for 20 to 25 minutes until brilliant brown and set.
5. Allow cooling before serving.
6. Store the remaining servings at room temperature in an airtight container for up to 3 days.

Nutrition: Calories: 143 Cal - Fat: 9.5 g - Carbs: 11.2 g - Fiber: 1.8 g - Protein: 6 g

22. Blueberry Mary Jane Muffins

Ingredients:

- 1 cup of blueberries,
- fresh 1/3 cup of cannabis
- milk 1 egg, large
- 1/2 cup of cannabis oil
- 2 tsp. of baking powder
- 1/2 tsp. of salt, kosher
- 3/4 cup of sugar, granulated
- 1 ½ cups of flour, all-

PREPARATION: 20 MINUTES | COOKING: 30 MINUTES | SERVINGS: 24

purpose

Directions:

1. Preheat the broiler to 400F. Place paper liners in biscuit dish cups.

2. Combine the baking powder, salt, sugar and flour. Set them aside.

3. Place 1/2 cup of canna-oil into 1-cup estimating cup. Add marijuana milk and egg to fill the entire cup. Add this to the flour blend. Consolidate well.

4. Fold the blueberries into batter.

5. Fill biscuit cups with player. Sprinkle with cinnamon.

6. Bake for 15-20 minutes.

7. Serve warm.

Nutrition: Calories: 124 Cal | Fat: 7.8 g | Fiber: 3 g | Carbs: 300 g | Protein: 4 g

Chapter 9:   Marijuana Cakes Recipes

23. Banana Cake Bread

Ingredients:

- 1 tsp. baking soda
- 1/4 tsp. salt
- 1 tsp. of ground
- cinnamon 1 tbsp. of milk
- 1/2 cup of cannabutter
- 1/2 cup of chopped walnuts
- 3/4 cup of brown sugar
- 2 cups of flour (all-purpose works
- best) 2 eggs, beaten
- 3 large mashed overripe bananas

PREPARATION: 15 MINUTES | COOKING: 70 MINUTES | SERVINGS: 1 LOAF

Directions:

1. Set the stove to preheat at 350 degrees Fahrenheit (175 degrees C). Additionally, pause for a minute to lube a 9x5 inch skillet in anticipation of the bread.

2. Combine the dry fixings, the baking pop, cinnamon, flour and salt. Set aside.

3. Taking an alternate dish, cream together spread and earthy colored sugar. Add the bananas, eggs, milk, and pecans. Add the whole blend into the dry fixings and consolidate well.

4. Now the simple aspect. Basically take the hitter and empty it into the
   lubed skillet, baking it for 60 minutes (or until the toothpick test can be passed).

5. Make sure it cools for no less than ten minutes prior to endeavoring to move it out of the container, and cool totally prior to cutting.

Note: If you love banana and chocolate, this is delightful with ½ cup of choc chips added.

24. Cranberry Nut Loaf Cake

Ingredients:

- ½ tsp. baking soda
- ½ tsp. salt
- 1 ½ tsp. baking powder
- 1 tbsp. grated orange peel
- 1/4 cup of melted cannabutter
- 3/4 cup of granulated sugar
- 3/4 cup of coarsely chopped walnuts
- 3/4 cup of orange juice
- 1 cup of chopped cranberries (thawed or fresh)
- 2 cups of flour
- 1 egg, beaten

PREPARATION: **10 MINUTES** | COOKING: **60 MINUTES** | SERVINGS: **8 SLICES**

Directions:

1. Set the broiler to preheat at 350°F.
2. Take a huge bowl and blend the dry fixings (the baking pop, baking powder, flour, and salt). Consolidate with the cranberries and pecans, and set aside.
3. In an alternate dish, join the other fixings, blending great. Take the subsequent player and consolidate with the dry blend from previously, blending until only blended.
4. Here's that simple aspect, empty it into a baking skillet of decision (8x4, 9x5 work best). Set in the broiler and prepare for

around 60 minutes, it ought to have the option to breeze through the toothpick assessment when done.

5. When gotten done, permit cooling for no less than 10 minutes prior to removing it from the pan.

6. Note: If you love cranberries and need a prettier bread, sprinkle a few entire cranberries on top of the player before you heat it. The blast of red on top adds a flawless appearance and flavor to the bread.

7. If you can't find fresh or frozen cranberries, you can use dried fruit instead. Just soak them in orange juice or water 30 – 60 mins first.

Nutrition: Calories: 237 Cal - Fat: 11 g - Carbs: 31 g - Fiber: 5 g - Protein: 6 g

25. Tres Leche Cake

Ingredients:

- 1/2 tsp. vanilla extract
- 1 tsp. baking powder
- 1/2 cup cannabutter
- 1 cup white sugar
- 1 ½ cups of flour (all-purpose works
- best) 1 ½ cups of heavy whipping cream
- 2 cups whole
- milk 5 eggs
- 12 fluid ounces of evaporated milk
- 14 ounces of sweetened condensed milk

PREPARATION: 30 MINUTES | COOKING: 30 MINUTES | SERVINGS: 24

Directions:

1. Prepare a 9x13 baking dish by lubing it and saving it. Set the oven to preheat at 350 degrees Fahrenheit.
2. In one dish, filter the dry fixings together (baking powder and flour).
3. Using an alternate dish, blend the cannabutter and sugar until velvety. Now, it's the ideal opportunity for the vanilla and the eggs, try to mix them in well.
4. Remember that dry blend? Add it in two tablespoons by two tablespoons, guaranteeing everything gets joined completely before

   moving to the baking dish.
5. Cook for around 30 minutes.
6. Remove the cake skillet to a cooling rack and permit to cool for 30 minutes. Jab the highest point of the cake done with a stick or fork and permit it to cool completely.
7. Now it's the ideal opportunity for the final details. Blend the milk(s) and top the cake with those first. The icing (a blend of the whipped cream, the sugar, and the vanilla) goes on last, a thick reward to a delightful cake.
8. Chill and keep refrigerated until prepared to serve.

Nutrition: Calories: 428 Cal - Fat: 25 g - Carbs: 44 g - Fiber: 1 g - Protein: 8 g

26. Blueberry and Apple Cookie Cake

Ingredients:
Crust

Filling

1/3 cup of sugar 1/2 cup cannabutter

1 cup of flour (universally handy works best)

- 1/2 tsp. cinnamon
- 3/4 tsp. baking powder
- 1 tsp. vanilla
- 1 cup fresh blueberries (thaw if using frozen)
- 1 cup apple, peeled, cored and thinly sliced
- 2/3 cup of granulated sugar
- 1/4 cup of brown sugar, firmly packed
- 1/4 cup of flour (all-purpose works best)
- 2 eggs

PREPARATION: 15 MINUTES | COOKING: 45 MINUTES | SERVINGS: 10

Directions:

1. Set the stove to preheat at 350°F.

2. Take a huge pot (or a huge medium) and spot over low-medium hotness. Utilize this to liquefy the cannabutter, blending it
ceaselessly for between 3-4 minutes. The outcome should be brilliant brown.

3. Once gotten done, take from the hotness right away. Join with 1 cup flour and 1/3 cup sugar; completely blending until it is fit to be put along the baking skillet (8-inch square works best). Press the blend into the base, and continue on to the following step.

4. Combine apple, blueberries, flour, baking powder, cinnamon, sugar, and vanilla. Add the eggs, beating until smooth, and use on the newly heated covering. Wrap the set up by sprinkling the earthy colored sugar, and spot in the broiler to bake.

5. Baking time is around 40-45 minutes. The top should finish a toothpick assessment, and give off an impression of being a sound brilliant. Allow it to chill off before cutting.

6. Serve on its own or with a good quality vanilla ice cream or whipped cream.

27. Dried Cherry and Almond Mini Loaf Cake

Ingredients:

- 1/4 tsp. ground cloves
- 1 tsp. baking soda
- 1 tsp. salt
- 1 tsp. vanilla
- 2 tsp. baking
- powder 1 tbsp. honey
- 2 tbsp. of brown sugar, firmly packed
- 1 cup of sugar
- 1 cup buttermilk
- 1 cup roughly chopped almonds
- 1 cup dried cherries
- 3/4 cup cannabutter, softened
- 3 cups of flour (all-purpose works best)
- 2 eggs
- 1/2 cup of chocolate chips

Cherry Butter

- 1 tsp. almond extract

- 2 tbsp. powdered sugar
- 1/2 cup of cherry preserves
- 1 cup cannabutter, softened (or regular butter as cannabutter is in the loaves)

PREPARATION: 20 MINUTES | COOKING: 35 MINUTES | SERVINGS: 5 MINI-LOAVES

Directions:

1. Set the stove to preheat to 350°F.
2. Mix the dry fixings in a bowl and set aside for the time being (baking powder, baking pop, cloves, flour, salt).
3. In an alternate dish, blend the leftover fixings - saving the almonds, the cherries, and the chocolate chips - trying to add the eggs just each in turn. The hitter ought to be velvety and smooth.
4. Gradually add the flour combination and beat tenderly until completely joined. Presently it's an ideal opportunity to add those chocolate chips, cherries, and almonds. The explanation they're put something aside for last is to guarantee they can be equitably distributed.
5. Take the subsequent hitter and scoop into five very much lubed scaled down portion dish (5 ½ x 3-inch).
6. Cook until it can breeze through the toothpick assessment, around half-hour - 40 minutes. Let cool for 15 mins prior to moving to a wire rack to cool completely.
7. While cooling, cream 1 cup of butter/cannabutter and some preserves. This makes a delicious topping for your bread!

Nutrition: Calories: 268 Cal - Fat: 10 g - Carbs: 38 g - Fiber: 3 g - Protein: 7 g

28. Simple One-Pan Lemon Cake

Ingredients:

Cake

-
-
-
-
-
-
-
-

Glaze

1/2 tsp. salt

1 ½ tsp. baking powder

2 tsp. newly ground lemon zing 1/4 cup

of cannabutter

3/4 cup of milk 1 cup of

sugar

1 ¼ cups of flour (generally useful) 1

Egg

- 1 tbsp. of melted cannabutter
- 3/4 cup of powdered sugar
- 2-3 tsp. lemon juice
- Lemon zest (optional)

PREPARATION: 15 MINUTES | COOKING: 30 MINUTES | SERVINGS: 9

Directions:

1. Set the stove to preheat to 350°F.
2. Prepare a 8x8 baking skillet by lubing it. Add the dry fixings (the baking powder, flour, salt, and sugar) to the baking container itself, making an opening in the middle.
3. Now, taking a bowl, consolidate the lemon zing and the egg, stirring
   with a fork. Empty the outcome into the opening you made, and add the softened cannabutter into the equivalent place.
4. Finally, pour the milk over the whole blend and mix thoroughly.
5. All that is left is to prepare it for roughly a half-hour. Whenever it's done, a toothpick should be perfect and dry when dunked in. Haul it out of the broiler and permit it to cool completely.
6. While it's cooling, blend 1 more tablespoon of cannabutter with

lemon squeeze and powdered sugar to make a frosting and coat the cake with it.

7. Enjoy!

Nutrition: Calories: 172 Cal - Fat: 5 g - Carbs: 30 g - Fiber: 4 g - Protein: 3 g

29. World Famous Chocolate Hash Cake

Ingredients:

- 225 g dark chocolate
- 225 g cannabis butter
- 345 g caster sugar, plus a pinch of
- extra 6 eggs, separated into yolks and
- whites 120 g ground almonds
- 145 g soft white breadcrumbs
- 30 g of flour
- 4 teaspoons of vanilla essence

For the icing

- 85 g cocoa
- powder 225 g
- icing sugar 130 g
- of butter 170 g
- caster sugar 6

PREPARATION: 30 MINUTES | COOKING: 10 MINUTES | SERVINGS: 5

tbsp. water

Directions:

1. Preheat the stove to 160 ° C/gas mark 3. Oil and line a 24 cm round cake tin.

2. For the space cake: liquefy the chocolate in a twofold evaporator or a bowl over a container of bubbling water.

3. Beat the weed margarine with 345 g sugar until it is pale and soft.

4. Beat in the egg yolks steadily and mix in the almonds. Overlap in the cool dissolved chocolate, breadcrumbs, flour and vanilla extract.

5. In a different bowl, beat the egg whites with a touch of sugar until solid however not dry. Overlay in the cake combination and fill the pre-arranged cake pan.

6. Bake for 1 hour until firm to the touch.

7. For the icing: sifter the cocoa and powdered sugar in a bowl.

8. Heat the margarine, sugar and water in a microwave or twofold evaporator and stew until the sugar is dissolved.

9. Add the fluid to the dry blend and join until thickened.

10. Divide the icing over the cooled hash cake.

Nutrition: Calories: 89 Cal - Fat: 2.6 g - Carbs: 13.7 g - Fiber: 0 g - Protein: 0.1 g

30. Cannabis Cheesecake

Ingredients:

- 1 tsp. of vanilla extract, pure
- 1/4 cup of lemon juice, fresh
- 1 x 14-oz. can of condensed milk, sweetened
- 2 x 8-oz. pkg. of room temp cream cheese
- 1/3 cup of coconut oil, cannabis-infused
- 1 large pie crust, graham cracker, ready to use

Directions:

1. Beat cream cheddar and canna-coconut oil in a bowl until they are smooth.
2. Beat in dense milk, and scratch the sides of bowl to ensure you miss nothing. Beat in vanilla and lemon juice.
3. Pour filling into crust—smooth top. Cover with stretch wrap, refrigerate for two to three hours until it is firm. Add any toppings you like, then serve sliced.

Nutrition: Calories: 36 Cal - Carbs: 7.3 g - Fat: 0.4 g - Fiber: 1 g - Protein: 1.1g

Chapter 10: Cannabis Candies Recipes

31. Cannabis Hard Candy and Lollipop

Ingredients:
1 cup sugar

1/3 cup corn syrup

1/2 cup water

1/4 teaspoon cream of tartar

1/4 to 1 teaspoon seasoning

Li q uid food coloring

1 to 2 teaspoon (s) citric acid (optional)

3 tablespoons cannabis tincture

PREPARATION: 10 MINUTES | COOKING: 30 MINUTES | SERVINGS: 2

Directions:

1. Prepare either a marble piece or a upside-down cookie sheet (air under the sheet will help the candy to cool faster) by covering it with parchment paper and spraying it with oil. If you're using molds, prepare the molds with lollipop sticks, splash with oil, and place them on a cookie sheet or marble slab.

2. In your pan, over medium heat, mix together the sugar, corn syrup, water and cream of tartar with a wooden spoon until the sugar crystals dissolve.

3. Continue to mix, using a baked good brush dampened with warm water to break down any sugar crystals sticking to the sides of the container, then, at that point, stop blending as soon as the syrup starts to boil.

4. Place the candy thermometer in the pan, being cautious not to let it contact the base or sides, and let the syrup boil without mixing until the thermometer just comes to 300 degrees F (hard-crack stage).

5. Remove the skillet from the heat quickly, and let the syrup cool to about 275 degrees F before adding flavour, color, cannabis color and citrus acid (adding it sooner causes most of the flavour to

cook away). Caution

6. Be careful! The sugar syrup is extremely hot! If you consume yourself, run cold water over your hand for several minutes, yet do not apply ice.

7. Working q uickly, pour the syrup into the prepared molds and let cool for about 10 minutes. If you're not utilizing molds, pour small (2-inch) circles onto the prepared marble chunk or treat sheet, and place a lollipop stick in each one, twisting the stick to be sure it's covered with candy.

8. Let the candies cool for at least 10 minutes, until they are hard. Wrap separately in plastic wrap or cellophane and seal with tape or contort ties.

9. Store in a cool, dry place.

Nutrition: Calories: 76 Cal - Fat: 3.3 g - Carbs: 16.3 g - Fiber: 1.3 g - Protein: 0.4 g

32. Cannabis Toffee Candy

Ingredients:

- 2 cups roasted nuts (I like pecans)
- 1 cup sugar
- 1 cup butter (or cannabutter)
- 1 tablespoon light corn
- syrup 1/4 cup water
- 1 cup chocolate morsels

PREPARATION: 30 MINUTES | COOKING: 50 MINUTES | SERVINGS: 4

Directions:

1. Spread about 1 1/2 cups of chopped nuts on a non-stick

baking sheet (may need to lightly oil it, however not
excessively much).

2. Bring sugar, margarine and corn syrup to a boil over medium
   heat, blending constantly to forestall burning.

3. Cook until the combination peruses about 300 to 310 degrees and
   mixture is golden brown (use candy thermometer and work fast;
   once it reaches 300, there isn't a lot of time until it burns).

4. Pour sugar mixture over hacked nuts on the baking sheet. Spread
   chocolate over hot candy and spread with a spoon (chocolate will
   start liquefying as soon as it hits the candy).

5. Sprinkle the rest of the nuts over the highest point of the
   chocolate, and let the sheet cool for about 30 mins or until the
   candy is cool.

6. The candy should break apart pretty easily after it has cooled.

Nutrition: Calories: 48 Cal - Fat: 0.2 g - Carbs: 8.3 g - Fiber: 0.1 g - Protein: 0.3 g

33. Butterscotch Space Pops

Ingredients:

- 1 cup sugar
- ½ cup cannabis corn syrup
- 2 tablespoons water
- 1 ½ teaspoons vinegar
- ¼ cup cannabutter
- ¼ teaspoon vanilla extract

Directions:

1. Line baking sheet with waxed paper; set aside. Use cannabutter

to grease the sides of the saucepan.

2. Combine the sugar, cannabis corn syrup, water and vinegar. Cook over medium-high hotness for about 5 minutes, to boiling, blending continually with a wooden spoon to break up the sugar. Continue to cook the combination over medium heat, mixing continually, while adding the butter (cut into 8 pieces), 2 pieces at a time.

3. The candy mixture ought to boil at a moderate, steady rate over the whole surface. Wait for the candy thermometer to read 300 degrees. This should take 25 to 30 minutes.

4. Remove the saucepan from the heat. Mix in the vanilla extract. Cool for 5 minutes. Pour the combination, 1 to 2 tablespoons at a period, onto the lined baking sheets. The mixture will make 2 to 3 inch circles.

5. Quickly place a lollipop stick into each piece of candy, twisting gently to cover with the candy mixture. Let the lollipops harden. Wrap the lollipops individually in clear plastic wrap to store at room temperature.

Nutrition: Calories: 93 Cal - Fat: 4.2 g - Carbs: 13.4 g - Fiber: 1.3 g - Protein: 0.4 g

34. Peppermint Buddha Bark

Ingredients:

- 12 ounces white chocolate
- 6 ounces semisweet chocolate
- 4 tablespoons cannabis-infused coconut oil
- ½ teaspoon peppermint extract
-

3 candy canes (crushed)

Directions:

1. Line a 9×9 inch baking container with some material paper or aluminum foil, making sure to wrap the foil over the sides of the pan, and smooth out any wrinkles as you go. This step will guarantee a speedy clean up and will also allow for the peppermint bark to easily pop off the pan when it comes time to break it into individual pieces.

2. Melt together the semisweet chocolate chips and the white chocolate chips. To do this, create a twofold boiler using a heat-safe bowl and a saucepan filled with water. Choose a bowl that fits cozily over the top of the pot (Do not utilize a bowl that sits dubiously on top of the pot). You also want to ensure that the base of the bowl does not contact the water or you hazard consuming the chocolate.

3. As a aside, this recipe utilizes 3 layers of chocolate for the bark (white, semisweet, white). Feel free to switch up the q uantities of the chocolate and turn around the layering (semisweet, white, semisweet) if you so please!

4. Bring the water in the saucepan to a simmer, and place the heat-safe bowl containing your white chocolate chips over the sauce pan.

5. Melt the white chocolate chips until they're smooth.

6. Add in 4 tablespoons of cannabis-infused coconut oil and the ½ teaspoon of peppermint extract.

7. Stir until the two oils have fully dissolved into the white chocolate. Aside from curing the dish, the coconut oil will also create a decent

sparkle in the bark and allow it to have a decent "snap" when breaking up the pieces.

8. Once the liquefied white chocolate is smooth once more, pour half of it into the prepared pan. Slant the pan after you pour in half of the melted white chocolate to ensure an even covering/first layer.

9. Place the pan in the refrigerator and allow the first layer of chocolate to harden completely, about 30 minutes or so.

10. While your first layer of bark is setting, rehash the above steps in order to prepare a second double evaporator for your semi-sweet chocolate chips.

11. Once your semisweet chocolate chips are completely melted, eliminate the bowl from the twofold boiler.

12. Take the dish containing the first layer of white chocolate from the fridge and proceed to pour the entire bowl

of melted semisweet chocolate chips over the first layer. It is incredibly important that the initial layer of white chocolate is completely hardened, as introducing the subsequent layer will cause them to blend assuming that this is not the case.

13. Spread the second layer of semisweet chocolate chips evenly throughout the pan utilizing a spatula or baker's knife.

14. Place the pan back into the fridge as you wait for the second layer of chocolate to set, again roughly 30 minutes or so.

15. When the second layer of chocolate has set, add the third and final layer of white chocolate on top of the semisweet layer. Spread this third layer equitably with a spatula.

16. Place the candy canes into a Ziploc pack and proceed

to crush them into tiny pieces utilizing the back of a spoon or a rolling pin.

17.		Sprinkle the crushed candy sticks on top of the third and final layer of white chocolate covering the whole surface, and then place the pan back into the refrigerator until the bark is completely set (30 minutes to 1 hour).

18.		When ready to eat, remove the bark from the refrigerator and pull up on the sides of the aluminum foil - the bark should lift right out of the pan!

19.		Break the bark into individual pieces, and either package them up to give as a gift, or serve them to your guests immediately!

Nutrition: Calories: 93 Cal - Fat: 4.2 g - Carbs: 15 g - Fiber: 0.3 g - Protein: 0.3 g

35. Weed Cotton Candy

Ingredients:

- 2-3 weed candies
- 2 scoops flossine

PREPARATION: 10 Minutes | COOKING: 0 Minute | SERVINGS: 2

Directions:

1. Crush 2-3 weed candies using the mortar and pestle. Add flossine to the powder and pulverize it once more. Its important to ensure that the powdered candy is smooth and fine.

2. Next, the powdered mixture needs to be spun into candy with the assistance of the cotton candy machine. To utilize the candy machine correctly, it's important to set it on a consistent, flat

and smooth surface. Also, ensure that the machine is placed at a safe height, away from the reach of kids and pets. Once the important insurances are taken, the cotton candy machine is set to be used.

3. Once in place, turn on the sweets machine's mortar and fill the floss head with about 2 scoops of the candy-flossine mixture. You may need to make sure that you are not filling more than 90% of the floss head.

4. The secret to spinning the perfect cotton candy is getting the details right, beginning from the very starting until the absolute last step.

5. After about 30-40 seconds of turning on the heat, you will see strings of the candy forming in the machine. Plunge a lollipop stick inside and gather the cotton candy by spinning the stick around. Do not rotate the stick itself, yet move it in a circular motion instead. Avoid touching the edges and turn off the machine once the cotton candy is done.

6. After a couple of trials, you'll be able to spin the perfect weed cotton candy, much to the amazement of those around you!

Nutrition: Calories: 91 Cal - Fat: 3.6 g - Carbs: 13.6 g - Fiber: 1.1 g - Protein: 0.2 g

36. Cannabis Hard Candy

Ingredients:

- 1 cup cannabutter
- 2 cups white sugar
- ¾ cup water
- ¼ cup honey

- ½ cup corn or rice syrup
- ½ teaspoon sea salt
- 1 teaspoon vanilla or almond extract
- 2 tablespoons regular butter or coconut oil

PREPARATION: 10 MINUTES | COOKING: 15-20 MINUTES | SERVINGS: 5

Directions:

1. Heat your honey and cannabutter to the point that they're in a li q uid, pourable state. Set aside.
2. Use the regular butter or coconut oil to coat your candy molds.
3. Heat sugar, water and corn/rice syrup in a pot. Cover without mixing and bring to a boil.
4. Once the combination is boiling, use a candy thermometer to check heat until the temperature reaches 132°C, the "soft-crack" stage. This ought to take about 15 minutes past the place of boiling.
5. Stir in cannabutter, salt and honey and continue heating until the mixture arrives at 148°C. This is the "hard-break" stage, and now the blend should bubble to the edges of the pot.
6. Turn off the heat, wait for the bubbles to subside, and stir in the vanilla or almond extract.
7. Pour the mixture into the molds. On the off chance that you're using candy sticks, place one end in the mold with the candy.
8. Allow the candy to cool for 30-an hour. Press the candy out of the molds afterward.
9. Wrap the candy in aluminum foil or wax paper and refrigerate.

Nutrition: Calories: 86 Cal - Fat: 3.2 g - Carbs: 12.3 g - Fiber: 1 g - Protein: 0.1 g

Chapter 11: Marijuana Ice-cream Recipes

37. Very Berry Cheesecake Ice Cream Pops

Ingredients:

- 4 ounces low-fat cream cheese
- 3/4 cup plain yogurt
- 1/4 cup agave syrup
- 1 teaspoon lemon or lime juice
- 2 gram decarboxylated kief or finely ground decarboxylated hash
- 3/4 cup fresh raspberries
- 3/4 cup fresh blueberries

PREPARATION: 10-15 MINUTES | COOKING: 0 MINUTE | SERVINGS: 4

Directions:

1. Make the cream cheddar light and soft utilizing a stand blender or a hand mixer.
2. Using the low speed, include agave syrup, yogurt, lime or lemon juice until it consolidated well.
3. Next, crease in the berries utilizing an elastic spatula.
4. Put the combination into Popsicle shape then, at that point, put them in the freezer.

Nutrition: Calories: 200 Cal - Fat: 5.9 g - Carbs: 54.6 g - Fiber: 2.1 g - Protein: 1.1 g

38. Mango Yogurt Ice Cream Pops

Ingredients:

- 3 tbsp. coconut sugar
- 2 mangoes, peeled and
- cut 3 tbsp. canna coconut
- oil 2 cups vanilla yogurt
- 2 tsp. coconut extract

Directions:

1. Toss in every one of the fixings in the blender.
2. Puree until it frames a smooth mix.
3. Transfer blend into Popsicle molds.
4. Freeze molds.

Nutrition: Calories: 210 Cal - Fat: 7 g - Carbs: 43 g - Fiber: 2 g - Protein: 2.1 g

39. Nutty Banana Yogurt Ice Cream Pops

Ingredients:

1½ cups vanilla yogurt

¼ cup unsweetened cocoa powder

1 tablespoon Canna-Coconut Oil

1 ready medium banana, cut and frozen

1 tablespoon honey

½ cup chopped peanuts

PREPARATION: 10 MINUTES | COOKING: 0 MINUTE | SERVINGS: 6

Directions:

1. In a blender, purée the yogurt, cocoa, canna-coconut oil, banana, and honey until smooth.
2. Put the mix into one more bowl and blend in the peanuts.
3. Pour the blend into Popsicle forms and freeze until firm.
4. Remove the flies from the molds as per the producer's instructions.

5. Storage: Keep the pops in an airtight container in the freezer for up to several months.

40. Double Chocolate Gelato Ice Cream

Ingredients:

- 1/2 cup heavy cream
- 2 cups of milk
- 3/4 cup sugar
- 1/4 teaspoon salt
- 7 ounces high-quality dark chocolate
- 1 teaspoon vanilla extract
- Cannabis butter

PREPARATION: 15-20 MINUTES | COOKING: 5-10 MINUTES | SERVINGS: 4-6

Directions:

1. The initial step is finished by softening the chocolate, then, at that point, cooling it for a bit.
2. Place the milk, cream, and weed spread in a bowl and blend them until all around joined. Blend in the sugar by utilizing a whisk and salt. Keep on rushing for around 4 minutes until the sugar and salt dissolve.
3. Then blend in the vanilla concentrate. At last, blend in the chocolate until well combined.
4. Pour the fixings into your frozen yogurt creator, and let it agitate for 25 minutes.

5. Put the gelato in a sealed shut holder and spot in cooler for up to
    2 hours, until wanted consistency is reached.

Nutrition: Calories: 230 Cal - Fat: 9 g - Carbs: 60.1 g - Fiber: 5.4 g - Protein: 4 g

41. Canna Cherry-Strawberry Gelato Ice Cream

Ingredients:

- 1/2 cup heavy cream
- 2 cups of milk
- 3/4 cup sugar
- Cannabis butter
- 1 cup sliced strawberries
- 1 tablespoon vanilla extract

PREPARATION: 20 MINUTES | COOKING: 0 MINUTE | SERVINGS: 4-6

Directions:

1. Using a blender, puree the strawberry thoroughly.
2. Place the milk, cream, and pot margarine in a bowl and blend
    them until well combined.
3. Mix in the sugar by utilizing a whisk. Keep on rushing for
    around 4 minutes until the sugar dissolves.
4. Then blend in the vanilla concentrate and strawberry puree.
5. Pour the fixings into your frozen yogurt producer, and let it stir
    for 25 minutes.
6. Put the gelato in an airtight container and place in the freezer for 2
    hours, until desired consistency is reached.

Nutrition: Calories: 210 Cal - Fat: 6.8 g - Carbs: 34.6 g - Fiber: 6 g - Protein: 3 g

42. Peaches-N-Cream Soft Serve Ice Cream

Ingredients:

- 2 cups heavy
- cream 1 cup milk
- 3⁄4 cup sugar
- Cannabis butter
- 1 Tbs. vanilla
- extract 1 cup sliced

PREPARATION: 35 MINUTES | COOKING: 0 MINUTE | SERVINGS: 4-6

peaches

Directions:

1. Using a blender, puree the peaches thoroughly.
2. Place the milk, cream, and weed margarine in a bowl and blend them until well combined.
3. Mix in the sugar by utilizing a whisk. Keep on rushing for around 4 minutes until the sugar dissolves.
4. Then blend in the vanilla concentrate. Then, at that point, blend in the peaches.
5. Put every one of the pre-arranged fixings in a perfect frozen yogurt producer and let it stir for 25 minutes.
6. Serve immediately.

Nutrition: Calories: 240 Cal - Fat: 6 g - Fiber: 2 g - Carbs: 56 g - Protein: 1.5 g

43. Tropical Mango Soft Serve Ice Cream

Ingredients:

- 2 cups heavy
- cream 1 cup milk
- 3⁄4 cup sugar
- 1 Tbs. vanilla extract
- 1 cup pureed mango (about 2.5 mangos)
- Juice of 1 lime
- Cannabis butter

PREPARATION: 35 MINUTES | COOKING: 0 MINUTE | SERVINGS: 6

Directions:

1. Puree the mangos with the lime juice in a food processor
   or blender.
2. Place the milk, cream, and weed margarine in a bowl and blend
   them until well combined.
3. Use a race to blend in the sugar. Keep on racing for around 4
   minutes until the sugar dissolves.
4. Then blend in the vanilla concentrate. Then, at that point, blend in
   the mango puree.
5. Put every one of the pre-arranged fixings in a spotless frozen
   yogurt creator and let it beat for 25 minutes.
6. Serve immediately.

Nutrition: Calories: 176 Cal - Fat: 2.1 g - Fiber: 6 g - Carbs: 36 g - Protein: 0.4 g

44. Lime Coconut Ice Pops

Ingredients:

- 1 ¼ ounces canna coconut milk,
- canned 1 cup cream

- 2 tablespoons limeade
- concentrate 1 tablespoon lime
  zest
- 2 tablespoons lemon juice
- Pinch of salt

PREPARATION: 10 MINUTES | COOKING: 0 MINUTE | SERVINGS: 4

Directions:

1. Toss in every one of the fixings in the blender.
2. Puree until it shapes a smooth mix.
3. Transfer blend into Popsicle molds.
4. Freeze molds.

Nutrition: Calories: 180 Cal - Fat: 2.5 g - Fiber: 8 g - Carbs: 35.9 g - Protein: 0.2 g

45. Rose Coconut Ice Cream

Ingredients:

- ⅓ Cup Rose Tea
- 2 ¾ cup canna cream
- 10 egg yolks
- 5 tablespoons Simple Syrup
- 1 cup coconut, shredded

PREPARATION: 15 MINUTES | COOKING: 10-15 MINUTES | SERVINGS: 4-6

Directions:

1. In a twofold evaporator heat until almost bubbling and eliminate from the hotness rose tea and cream.
2. In a different bowl, race until foamy eggs and milk.

3. Pour the warm milk over the eggs whisking ceaselessly, then, at that point, once again into the skillet over low heat.
4. Cook and mix until the combination thickens.
5. The blend should be stressed to a perfect bowl and add coconut.
6. Cover with cling wrap and cool at room temperature.
7. Pour into an electric ice cream machine and follow the manufactures direction.

46. Chai Green Tea Ice Cream

Ingredients:

- 2 cups heavy cream
- 2 Chai Tea Blend, dry
- 6 egg yolks
- 1 cup of the warm cream
- ¼ cup instant coffee granular
- 3 tablespoons stevia
- 3 tablespoons canna sugar
- 2 teaspoons vanilla
- ½ cup Chai Tea

Directions:

1. Mix everything in less than a twofold heater and hotness up gradually.
2. Once the blend is smooth and sort of thick, eliminate from hotness and cool down.

3. After this, put in the frozen yogurt producer and churn.

4. Transfer to a holder and freeze.

Chapter 12: Other Cannabis Dessert Recipes

47. Danish Puffs

Ingredients:

- 1/8 tsp. salt

- 1/2 cup of cannabutter

- 1 cup of all-purpose flour

- 1 cup water

- 4 eggs

PREPARATION: 15 MINUTES | COOKING: 30 – 35 MINUTES | SERVINGS: 10 - 12

Directions:

1. Turn the stove on and preheat to the tune of 350°F.

2. Take a rock solid pan (2 quarts) and join the cannabutter, salt, and water.

3. Heat the pot over medium hotness to the mark of boiling.

4. At the principal indication of a full bubble, start to add the flour. Mix ceaselessly for around sixty seconds, until a ball forms.

5. Take the pan off of the hotness source and permit it to cool.

6. Add every one of the eggs in, blending after every one is added. The subsequent blend ought to be incredibly smooth.

7. Take the batter in tablespoons and spot onto an ungreased baking sheet, making a point to leave something like 3 crawls between each portion.

8. Place in the stove and cook until gently brilliant and puffed, around thirty minutes. When gotten done, jab each puff with a fork; this will assist it with chilling faster.

9. Once totally chilled, eliminate the tops and any delicate mixture remainders. Add your preferred filling, finish it off with some warm chocolate chips, powdered sugar, or cocoa and enjoy!

10. Fillings that will make your mouth water:

11.   There's a lot of flexibility here, the best fillings tend to be frozen (frozen yogurt, sorbet, ice cream), but there are also warm fillings (pudding, pie filler, whipped cream). Don't forget to top!

48. Double Chocolate Pudding

Ingredients:

- 1 tbsp. Vanilla extract
- 2 tbsp. Cannabutter, cut into
- pieces 2 tbsp. Cornstarch
- 3 tbsp. Unsweetened cocoa
- powder 1/2 cup of white sugar
- 5 ounces of semisweet baker's chocolate, finely
- chopped 2 1/4 cups of whole milk
- 3 large egg yolks
- Just a pinch of
  salt
- Whipped cream for that special finishing touch!

PREPARATION: 5 MINUTES | COOKING: 15 MINUTES PLUS COOLING | SERVINGS: 6

Directions:

1. Take a medium pan and spot over medium hotness. Add the salt with half of the sugar and milk, persistently mixing over the hotness, and bring with the end result of bubbling. Once bubbled, remove the pot from the oven at once.
2. Take a bowl (separate from your pan) and join the cornstarch,

egg yolks, remaining milk, and add a spot of salt. Whisk completely and start to add the pan substance to the bowl.

3. Take that dependable and inclined toward pot and pour the substance of the bowl into it once more. Bring with the eventual result of bubbling over medium (high ought to likewise be fine here, simply don't allow it to consume) heat.

4. Take the hotness back down to a low level, to keep the substance of the pot stewing and rush for 2-3 minutes. The objective here is to thicken the pudding to wanted consistency. Whenever this is done, we can return to a bowl (hah!).

5. Depending on the sort of bowl utilized previously, you might need to snatch an alternate one, as you really want to guarantee that the substance of the pot just go into a heatproof bowl. Whenever you've done that, it's an ideal opportunity to add the cannabutter, vanilla, and chocolate into the dissolved combination of delight.

6. The subsequent pudding ought to be unquestionably, scrumptiously smooth, flavorful, and practically done. Set it up for capacity (It can be put away all in all, however I like to isolate it - makes around six servings), and chill it short-term to set the pudding.

7. That's it; it's ready for your final touch of choice! Mine, of course, is whipped cream.

Nutrition: Calories: 91 Cal - Fat: 5.6 g - Protein: 2.9 g - Fiber: 0 g - Carbs: 13.4 g

49. Strawberry Jam Cannabis Crepes

Ingredients:

- 3 eggs
- 1/4 cup sugar
- 2 cups plain flour
- 2 cups of milk
- 1/2 stick cannabis-infused butter
- 1 large orange, juiced
- 1/2 tsp. vanilla
- 1/4 cup sunflower oil
- 1/2 cup strawberry jam

PREPARATION: 10 MINUTES | COOKING: 15-20 MINUTES | SERVINGS: 10

Directions:

1. Using an electric blender daintily beat eggs and 1/4 cup sugar on medium speed until very much consolidated. Add 1/2 cup flour, 1 tablespoon at an at once, after every option. Gradually add staying 1 1/2 cups flour and milk on the other hand until hitter is smooth. Decrease blender speed to medium-low. Add 1/2 cup squeezed orange, vanilla and a touch of salt. Beat until hitter is smooth.

2. Heat a 7-inch base crêpe skillet or griddle over medium hotness. Brush dish with a little oil. Pour 2 1/2 tbsp hitter into focus of dish and whirl to cover base. Cook for 1 to 2 minutes or until the base is

   brilliant. Turn and cook for 30 seconds. Move to a plate, put 3D squares of spread in the middle hot crêpes. Rehash with outstanding hitter, lubing container between crêpes.

3. Spread one teaspoon of jam over one crêpe. Roll crêpe up tightly.

Nutrition: Calories: 87 Cal - Fat: 3.6 g - Carbs: 12.1 g - Fiber: 1 g - Protein: 0.4 g

Repeat with remaining crêpes and jam. Layer crêpes on a serving plate. Serve sprinkled with powdered sugar.

50. Cannabis Baked Apples

Ingredients:

- 8 medium-sized apples
- 1/3 cup walnuts, crushed
- 3/4 cup sugar
- 3 tbsp. raisins, soaked
- Vanilla, cinnamon according to taste
- 1 stick cannabis-infused butter

PREPARATION: 8 MINUTES | COOKING: 13 MINUTES | SERVINGS: 4

Directions:

1. Peel and cautiously empty the apples. Plan stuffing by beating margarine, 3/4 cup of sugar, squashed pecans, raisins and cinnamon.
2. Stuff the apples and spot in an oiled dish, pour more than 1-2 tbsp of water and prepare in a moderate stove. Serve warm with a scoop of vanilla ice cream.

Nutrition: Calories: 232 Cal - Carbs: 27 g - Fat: 12.5 g - Protein: 3.4 g - Fiber: 33 mg

51. Pumpkin Cannabis Pastry

Ingredients:

- 14 oz. filo pastry
- 1 cups pumpkin, shredded

- 1/2 stick cannabis-infused butter 1 cup walnuts, coarsely chopped 1/2 cup sugar
- 6 tbsp. sunflower oil
- 1/2 tbsp. ground cinnamon
- 1 tsp. vanilla extract
- 5-6 tbsp. powdered sugar

PREPARATION: 10 MINUTES | COOKING: 15-20 MINUTES | SERVINGS: 8

Directions:

1. Grate the pumpkin and steam it until delicate. Add margarine and consolidate with the pecans, sugar, cinnamon and vanilla. Cook together until sugar has begun caramelizing.
2. Place a couple of sheets of baked good in the baking dish, sprinkle with oil and spread the filling on top while still warm. Rehash this a couple of times, wrapping up with a sheet of pastry.
3. Bake for 20 minutes at 350 F. Let the Pumpkin Pie cool down and dust with the powdered sugar.

Nutrition: Calories: 302 Cal - Carbs: 27 g - Fat: 12.5 g - Protein: 3.7 g - Sodium: 33 mg

52. Baklava-Walnut Pie

Ingredients:

- 14 oz. filo pastry
- 1 cup ground walnuts
- 3 sticks cannabis-infused butter

For the syrup:

- 2 cups sugar
- 2 cups water
- 1 tbsp. vanilla powder
- 2 tbsp. lemon zest

PREPARATION: 10 MINUTES | COOKING: 30-45 MINUTES | SERVINGS: 15

Directions:

1. Grease a baking plate and spot 2-3 sheets of baked good. Pulverize the pecans and spread some uniformly on the baked good. Place two additional sheets of the filo baked good on top. Rehash until all the baked good sheets and pecans have been spent. Continuously get done for certain sheets of cake on top.

2. Cut the pie in the plate into little squares. Soften the margarine and pour it over the pie. Heat in a preheated broiler at 350 F until light brown. Whenever prepared, put away to cool.

3. The syrup: Combine water and sugar in a pot. Add vanilla and lemon zing and bring to the bubble, then, at that point, bring down the hotness and

   simmer for about 5 minutes until the syrup is nearly thick. Pour hot syrup over the cold baked pie. Leave to stand for at least 1-2 days until completely dry.

Nutrition: Calories: 232 Cal - Carbs: 23 g - Fiber: 3.3 g - Fats: 17 g - Protein: 3.6 g

53. Canna Choco Dipped Strawberries

Ingredients:

1 ½ cups chocolate chips

2 tablespoons cannabis-coconut
oil 12 strawberries

PREPARATION: 5 MINUTES | COOKING: 2-4 MINUTES | SERVINGS: 5-6

Directions:

1. In a medium-sized bowl, completely blend the coconut oil and chocolate chips.
2. Set the microwave on high, and hotness the combination for 30-40 seconds. Take it out and mix well.
3. Place it back and warm it for 15-20 additional seconds, and afterward mix once more, rehashing until the blend is impeccably smooth.
4. Let it cool down for 10 minutes.
5. Dip the new strawberries into the chocolate mixture.
6. Place them on a piece of material paper, and keep far away from children.
7. Let sit for 20 minutes to set, and serve.

Nutrition: Calories: 232 Cal - Carbs: 27 g - Fat: 12.5 g - Protein: 3.4 g - Fiber: 3.3 g

54. Cannabis Honey Oats

Ingredients:

- 1 ½ cups cannabutter
- 2 tablespoons cocoa powder
- ½ cup peanut butter
- 3   tablespoons
- honey 8 cups rolled

PREPARATION: 8-10 MINUTES | COOKING: 5 MINUTES | SERVINGS: 6-7 oats

Directions:

1. Spray a baking sheet with cooking shower and set it aside.
2. Melt the margarine in a pot over medium heat.
3. Add the excess fixings one by one.
4. Mix well and hotness the combination for 2-3 minutes.
5. Spread the combination in the baking container and chill for 18-20 minutes.
6. Form the oats into medium-sized balls, and chill for another a large portion of an hour.
7. Serve cold!

Nutrition: Calories: 494 Cal - Carbs: 77 g - Fat: 14.5 g - Protein: 17 g - Fiber: 2 g

55. Strawberries with Honey Cream

Ingredients:

- 1 cup plain, low-fat Greek
- yogurt 1 tablespoon honey
- 2 teaspoons canna-oil (here)
- ½ teaspoon vanilla extract
- 1 cup fresh strawberries, cleaned and sliced

PREPARATION: 10 MINUTES | COOKING: 20 MINUTES | SERVINGS: 2

Directions:

1. In a little bowl, consolidate the yogurt, honey, canna-oil, and vanilla. Utilizing an electric blender or whisk, beat for 3 to 4 minutes until fluffy.
2. Divide the strawberries between 2 dishes and top with

equivalent bits of the honey cream.

3. Serve when prepared to eat.

4. Store the leftover serving in an impenetrable holder in
    the cooler for up to 3 days.

5. You can use any type of fruit in place of the strawberries. The
    honey cream is also quite delicious with orange segments and
    walnuts.

Nutrition: Calories: 126 Cal - Fat: 5.8 g - Carbs: 11.7 g - Fiber: 1.4 g - Protein: 5.3g

56. Apple Pie Bars

Ingredients:

- 1/2 Cup Cannabis Butter at room temperature
- 3/4 cup sugar
- 2 eggs
- 1 tbsp. vanilla
- 1 1/2 cup flour
- 3/4 tsp. baking powder
- 1 tbsp. apple pie spice
- 2 Cup apple pie filling

PREPARATION: **10 MINUTES** | COOKING: **40 MINUTES** | SERVINGS: **12**

Directions:

1. Cream spread; add sugar and beat well. Beat in eggs each in turn.
    Add vanilla.

2. Gradually mix in filtered dry ingredients.

3. Spread ¾ of mixture in a softly lubed 8x11 inch baking pan.

4. Spread fruity dessert filling over dough.

5. Spoon remaining batter over pie filling, spreading daintily. (Not all pie filling will be covered.)

6. Bake at 375 degrees for 35-40 minutes.

Conclusion

Thank you for coming as far as possible. These plans are straightforward and simple to make at home. Marijuana has been found to effectsly affect the human body whenever taken in a controlled sum. We have clinical proof to demonstrate the abovementioned. Consequently, the world over the spice has tracked down a spot in the eating routine. In each culture, however it isn't essential for the ordinary diet.

Use marijuana assuming you seriously love it. There are alternate approaches to remembering it for the eating routine. Canna-implanted oil to prepare food things that can be cooked in low hotness is the least demanding way.

Marijuana or weed is exactly the same thing. It is consumed the world over for its capacity to get individuals on a high. Nonetheless, it is to be noticed that individuals get high from smoking it. But the weed gives better results when eaten. Oral utilization invests in some opportunity to show its belongings, yet the impacts are stronger.

For an hour or something like that, there won't get a response. It begins just later and may keep going for quite a long time. Smoking pot is illicit, however eating it in little amounts probably won't land you in jail. But you still may be caught for its possession.
Be careful.

If you need extreme impacts, eat weed. Discover ways of adding it to your ordinary stuff. There are various ways of doing as such. Add it to the milk, however you should bubble it for an hour or so to get the impact. Drink it quickly or store it in the refrigerator. Would you be able to remember it for your treats or brownies? These are ordinary sorts of stuff that you eat around the home.

Eating it very well might be just about as unlawful as smoking it, however assuming you have a cake stacked with pot, you are less inclined to be caught.

No big surprise the US President Clinton never smoked hash. The other significant highlight note about it is that weed is required distinctly in little amounts. It in any case tastes awful.

It will help assuming that you sprinkle the spice uniformly over the food you are getting ready. Since we are searching for THC to enter our circulatory system, adding it to light food sources is the most ideal way. Else it might take more time for it to enter the bloodstream.

In Asian cooking, there is explained spread or ghee, which infers the advantages of marijuana. Recollect not to consume the ghee or oil. When it softens, add the finely powdered marijuana. Keep the hotness low when cooking.

The other significant point is that cook a few things of a similar size to monitor the extent. Since you don't quantify the marijuana prior to sprinkling it, we don't have any idea the amount we have added. One treat might have a greater amount of it while another may have less. That will bring about the impact likewise fluctuating. Assuming you eat one and see nothing even following an hour or so has passed, take a stab at eating another. This isn't the most ideal way to eat the stuff.

Use chocolate to blend the powdered spice. Be that as it may, make certain to warm it prior to sprinkling it. Its power must be mixed after it is warmed. The THC in it stays unaffected in any case, and you may not get the ideal high.

Have fun!